MW00626265

What
Is
This
Thing
Called

"I"?

What Is This Thing Called "I"?

Allen Carter, Ph.D.

The Center for Self-Actualization, Inc.

Published by The Center for Self-Actualization, Inc.
Publishing Division
P.O. Box 98466
Atlanta, Georgia 30359
www.selfactualized.org

Copyright © 2005 by Allen C. Carter

Cover Designed by Graphic Gallery, Atlanta, Georgia

Library of Congress Cataloging in Publication Data

Carter, Allen C.
        What is this thing called I / by Allen C. Carter

ISBN 0-9758799-9-5

Printed in the United States of America

Without limiting the rights under copyright reserved above,
no part of this publication may be reproduced, stored in or
introduced into a retrieval system or transmitted in any form
or by any means (electronic, mechanical, photocopying,
recording or otherwise) without the expressed written
permission of the author. All rights reserved.

*Permission has been obtained from those depicted in this
book and the identities, circumstances and events have been
changed to protect the confidentiality of those involved.*

Dedication

To Robert and Ruth Carter, my first teachers in and of love. Thank you for providing me the opportunity and support to explore and investigate that which is good, that which is true, that which is eternal.

Acknowledgements

As this book clearly states, I am not a separate individual personality but instead I am ALL, including all the apparent identities that exist. To not acknowledge them all would be to not acknowledge myself. However, to enumerate each one that has contributed to me in this endeavor would probably take an entire book in and of itself.

Suffice it to say that I am truly grateful to all who have been in my life and continue to contribute to my growth and awareness as a spiritual being. I am especially grateful to my spiritual guides and teachers including Kay Causey, Joel Goldsmith and *A Course in Miracles*. Thank you all for being beacons forever shining forth the light of truth, love and forgiveness.

Contents

Part III
THE WAY OUT

The Introduction

So, what is this thing called I?

Is it a word or a letter in the alphabet? Is it a psychological term that refers to a human identity or is it something else? It seems so simple because it is a word that we use countless times each day. Every day we use it without considering the meaning. Yet, it may be more complex than the casual way we use it in our every day lives.

If we were truly to ask the question what does, "Who or what am I?" mean, an entire new world would open. For the question, **"Who am I?" is the most basic question of life**. It offers the key to discovering the answers to the most fundamental questions of life: creation, God, heaven and hell. It includes and transcends biology, sociology, philosophy, psychology and theology. It is what defines you, creates you, limits and expands you. The issue of identity is basic to the understanding of all life. For without you or I, there would be no awareness of life. And, if there is no awareness of life, could life exist?

The issue of identity is natural to psychologists. Often we invent other terms such as self-concept, ego and self-identity. These are well meaning terms but are primarily limited to a set of beliefs, ideas, emotions, and perceptions about a person. Identity has not been explored enough by the fields of biology, sociology, philosophy, psychology, or theology. As a result, the understanding of who we are is limited, and consequently, our awareness and knowledge of ourselves are limited.

As a professor at Morehouse College in Atlanta, this became clear to me. Over the past ten years, I have required students to write a term paper exploring, "Who am I?" Invariably, my students turned in papers that addressed their personal identities. They often began the paper by writing about their birth and how they coped with activities that stemmed from early childhood. This approach seemed to be the norm.

Before I gave them the assignment however, I would ask them to consider: What is the basis of your identity? Central to this question is the word **basis**, which means foundation or premise. I would further ask them to consider, on what grounds do you base your conclusion? The basis will determine any outcome. The basis is the source; it is the mother from which the idea is birthed. Without an understanding of the basis, one cannot fully understand the conclusion. In other words, without knowledge of the mother, one cannot fully understand or know the child.

Yet, it goes beyond knowing the basis. You can think you know the basis, but the basis can be false. And if the basis is false, then obviously the conclusion must also be false. To further explain, let me give you an illustration.

I once had a conversation with a colleague who was a fundamental Christian. His basic premise was, "The Bible is God's Word, and God's Word is True". I asked him if he could prove that everything written in the Bible was God's Word. He thought for a moment, and then confessed that he couldn't. I considered his confession to be nothing less than a great act of humility and a sign of wisdom. My question enabled him to see that his premise of the belief that the Bible is literally God's Word could be false, and thus, his conclusion could also be false. I assured him that I respected his beliefs and admired him for the convictions he held, and also for the devotion he showed to his faith. Nonetheless, the point remains, the premise, or as in this case, the basis, must be investigated if you want to know the Truth.

To discover the Truth, you must be willing to explore the premise of each fact uttered. You must be willing to tear that premise apart and go to any length to discover the Truth. For Truth is all there is.

"If it isn't the Truth then it is a lie – and no lie can live forever," said one great sage.

In order to discover the Truth, you must possess a determination and commitment to Truth, while also embracing a willingness to uncover unknown fears and anxieties. Once you begin this journey of Truth seeking, it becomes a journey within yourself. It is a journey into the inner recesses of the mind. It is a journey into "I."

Hence, to know yourself is to know the basis of your identity. It is the basis of knowing . . . "What is this thing called 'I'?"

Now, let's begin!

PART I

The Nature and Structure Of The Mind and Its Three Mental Gods

Chapter 1

The Meaning of "I" Versus "i"

As a child growing up in Normal, Alabama, I was fascinated with reading the Bible and books about biblical heroes. It was exciting to read about Moses leading his people out of the land of oppression to a promised land. The similarities between the oppressed people of Israel and black people in America were easy to see by a black child in the Jim Crow South in the 1950's. My interest was therefore personal and motivated by my race. I can vividly recall the passage of scripture when Moses encountered a burning bush and asked the bush to identify itself. The bush represented God, and it answered Moses' question with the self-description: "I Am That I Am."

God, as the story goes, used the term "I" to identify Himself. This fascinated me, although I didn't truly understand it. Now, being much older, I see that God took a word that most frequently refers to a personal identity, and made it a Universal Identity. "I" was no longer restricted to the identity of a human being. It applied to an Infinite Being, the Omnipotent and Omnipresent one, which is "I."

How can this be? How can "I" apply to you and me, while also applying to that which is Infinite, that which has no boundaries, that which is the Alpha and the Omega? The answer to this question contains all the problems and the solutions of the world. In this answer lie all the misery, suffering, hatred, love, joy, pain, and pleasure the world has known. The issue of identity and mistaken identity are both found in the answer.

If one accepts the premise that "I" is Infinite, and knows no limits or boundaries, then there can be no other I. The "I" that is Infinite can be the only "I." There cannot be two infinities. There cannot be two Infinite "I's." In this case there can only be one Infinity. In other words, there can only be one "I."

But, what of these other "I's" such as you and me and all the other six billion people in the world? How can this Infinite "I" and the other more personal "I" exist simultaneously? The premise of the question is, I as a human exist and accept that there is at least one other "I" that is Infinite and separate from me. This "I" is called the "I that I am." Throughout the remainder of this book we will refer to God, the "I Am," with a capital "I" and the lower case "i" will be used to classify the personal or human identity.

This "I Am" is boundless. It is complete. Yet, it seems to be apart or separate from me. And, herein lies the definition of a human. A human being has to be defined differently. Therefore, there is Infinity and "i", as stated in the often repeated cliché, "You and me, God." But is this possible? Can there be both Infinity and something else? To this personal "i" the answer is yes. For "i" know "i" exist as an individual. "i" do not have to prove it; "i" just know it.

Let's return to the premise: Infinity exists, but in order for me to exist as a human, "i" must be a finite being residing within Infinity or placed outside of Infinity. In other words, to be a human, "i" must believe that Infinity knows of limitation – its opposite. Therefore, a human, in order to exist, must limit or deny Infinity or God. Either way, the premise must now expand to include the concept of finite (me) and the opposite of finite – Infinite. The premise becomes more confusing and indeed contradictory. But, this is what appears to be my world, and dare "i" also say, your world.

To exist, man must believe that Infinity can have an opposite and that opposite can take the form of a human being. This, my friend, is the basis of human identity. This is the premise from which apparently all life has come and on which all life is based. Life is, therefore, formed on an incorrect or a self-contradicting premise. Is there no wonder that life is fraught with contradictions and errors? And it is never ending.

Assuming this premise is true, several questions remain: How did it come to be? How did the seemingly impossible occur? Did it really occur? If it did, does that mean that the impossible becomes the possible? Does it mean that all is God, including the opposite of God? Does it mean that the bad is God, and that the Devil is also God? Is that really possible? Does it make any sense at all? Each of these questions leads us on an adventure of untold wonders, an adventure that explores the deepest chambers of the mind – the creator of it all.

Chapter 2

Where Did "I" Come From?

I am in a process of self-discovery as I write this book. Memories of my childhood are arising like popcorn being popped in a movie theatre. I am consumed by even more recent memories of my adult years as a parent, trying to raise my two sons in a manner that I believed would help them become good and productive human beings. One of my childhood memories was sitting around the dinner table on Sunday after church. My role in the family was to be the smart aleck kid who asked my sisters and brother questions about the Bible. I asked the questions as a means of impressing my father. He was an educator and scientist and revered the process of intellectual inquiry. Although my motives were not so pure, my father, to the disgust of my brother and sisters, encouraged me to ask questions. This love of the inquiry was developed and became a special part of my personal identity.

As a parent, my sons questioned me, putting me on the other side of the table. I can recall the time, as I'm sure many parents do, of being asked: "Daddy, where did I come from?" I, of course, responded in the typical appropriate but evasive fashion common to many parents and supplemented my reply with the appropriate books. I wasn't aware at the time, how profound the question was. The "I", where did it come from? What is the origin of "I"? What is "I" and where did "I" – the "I" that is beyond human come from? In other words, what started it all?

Of course, the answer is simple: "i don't know." This answer usually doesn't end the questioning process. It usually leaves one begging – waiting for more. It is out of this wanting more that many theories have evolved: religious, scientific, meta-physical and even just plain crazy ones. So, what's to stop me from trying to add to the mix?

Realizing that "i", a finite being, don't know and cannot know of that which is Infinite, "i" am handicapped from the beginning. Yet, that doesn't necessarily have to preclude my going on this adventure and "i" invite you to come along. All you need to do is be open to all possibilities. I don't ask that you relinquish your reasoning process, be it deductive or inductive. In fact, bring them along and use them as primary tools of analysis as we ask this question that my sons asked of me: "Where did 'I' come from?"

Chapter 3

In The Beginning (The Universal Mind and The Creator-god)

For more than seven years I taught *Theories of Personality* at Morehouse College. Invariably, at the beginning of each semester I asked the students if they knew the definition of the word psychology. Most said psychology was the study of the mind. Others said it was the study of human behavior, and a few considered it to be the study of behavior, be it human or animal.

I remember a student named Jamal who asked, "What else could it be professor, besides the definitions we have given?" I smiled at Jamal and asked if he knew what the suffix "logy" meant?

"Of course," he said. "It means the study of."

"Very good," I replied. "And what does psyche mean?"

Jamal looked at me with some suspicion and said the word psyche meant mind.

"No," I said, with a smile. "Most people make the same mistake. So, don't feel bad Jamal, but the word psyche literally means soul. And, I'm not referring to soul as in soul-food or Soul-Brother!"

I searched Jamal's face as I continued, "The word soul, as Webster defines it, can mean essence. Psychology, therefore, actually means the study of the soul, or the essence."

Jamal soon figured out that he was in class to study the essence of who we are. I gave him a compliment, and said to accomplish that purpose I must start by teaching about the beginning of life.

Another student named Carl interrupted and asked, "What do you mean by the beginning of life? Are you talking about the creation of human life? If so, then you must be talking about the story of Adam and Eve in Genesis."

"Yes Carl, I am talking about the story of the very beginning, and I will include the story as related in Genesis, but I will also include other theories and explanations, including my own." I elaborated by saying I intended to explore: who am I and where did I come from. That also meant exploring the essence of me or "i".

Carl wished me luck, but said he preferred to stick with the Bible as the true story. I didn't want to be disrespectful of Carl's opinion or similar opinions shared by other students; so, I took a deep breath and said, "Carl, you are attending a liberal arts institution. As such you're in an environment that is structured to encourage open and scholarly inquiries into relevant issues and questions. I encourage you to hold on to your religious beliefs, but also to be open to the process of intellectual and scholarly pursuit of the unknown. If you can do that," I continued, "you may discover that the world has untold mysteries and answers that can take you on a journey that may be quite amazing."

"If you will allow me this position," I promised. "I will respect you and your beliefs, but I also offer you a possibility that there is a world beyond that which you are accustomed or familiar with."

Carl seemed to be reassured with my response. I told him I was glad he brought up the Book of Genesis and the story of Adam and Eve. "I think it says in Genesis that in the beginning God created the heavens and earth and the earth was without form. Now, even before anything was created, there had to be a presence or something. You may call it

God, but clearly it was an existence. It had no form because this was before any forms had been created. All we can assume is that it was without form but still was a presence."

"But wait a minute," interrupted Carl, "Are you saying God is formless, not a father figure in heaven?"

"What I'm saying Carl, is there is an existence that neither you nor I know of, because it is beyond anything conceivable by the human mind."

"Okay," said Carl. "I guess I'll grant you that professor, but go on. This is somewhat intriguing, although I don't know if it is true or not or if I can accept it or not."

"Carl," I said. "I'm not asking you to accept what I say as Truth about that which is unknowable or unexplainable. We can only speculate about it, and that is all I am doing. What I am saying is not necessarily true. It is only speculation that I hope will prompt you to ponder more and hence go to places in your mind that you have not gone before. That is all I want to do as your teacher."

"Okay, I can buy that professor. So, what happened next?"

"Good question," I replied. "Note that I said there is, or was a presence. What happened next was apparently, the impossible occurred."

"Impossible?" asked Carl.

"Yes, the impossible seemingly occurred as the Infinite Presence (All that is, was or ever will be) appeared to have a thought that something was separate from It. This of course is impossible because nothing can be apart from Infinity or Infinity would not be Infinite. By definition, Infinity is all that there is. Therefore there is nothing beyond or outside of Infinity. Yet, from our perspectives as humans, something happened and there was a separation from Infinity. (See Illustration I) I call this impossible act a thought because from our perspectives as humans, there is nothing outside of our thoughts. Otherwise we could not be aware of it."

"Whoa, hold your horses professor," said Carl. "Are you saying that God didn't create the universe?"

I paused before I responded. I knew how sensitive this situation was. I also knew the wrong answer could be explosive. So, I had to be careful and respectful.

"Carl," I said, "What we are talking about is starting with that which has no form or no creation and seeing if a world of form can be created from it. In other words, from your perspective as a human being, which relies upon forms that are created and perceived, we must consider if an understanding can be had of a world or dimension that is beyond perception.

Obviously, this is difficult, to say the least, and probably impossible at best. But, we as seekers of Truth must be open to this process. Surely, Carl, if there is an Infinite Presence that is formless and creates, that which it creates would still

Illustration #1

The Relationship Between Infinity, The Universal Mind And The Creator-god.

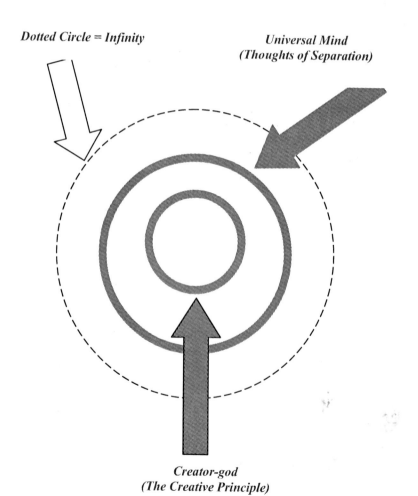

Dotted Circle = Infinity

**Universal Mind
(Thoughts of Separation)**

**Creator-god
(The Creative Principle)**

have to be within Infinity, because, by definition, nothing can be outside the realm of Infinity. But since we think we are separate from God or Infinity, then this separation appears to be our reality."

"Professor," interrupted Carl, "I think I can logically follow you, but this is so confusing."

I knew it was. I told Carl it had to be confusing because we were essentially talking about something that we had no direct knowledge of. No man knew or can know the mind of God or the Infinite. No human mind could grasp the Infinite. We could only speculate and hope that our speculation would open us up to learn more and accept what we learn.

"Hopefully, Carl, we can just be open to what emerges. At least that is my approach. Is that okay?"

"Well, I guess so, but this is rather upsetting."

"Yes," I replied, in what I hoped was a compassionate voice.

"To continue," I said, "it appeared as if there was a separation from the Infinite and this separation occurred in a form called thought. This thought or awareness of separation is what I call the universal mind.

The universal mind contains all that we know and are aware of. It began with the thought that there is at least one idea or one thought that is separate from another. This universal mind is equivalent to Descarte's pronouncement of, 'I think therefore I am.' Without thought, as Descarte said, "i" cannot exist or be. But, the "i" to which Descarte referred is not to be confused with the Infinite 'I' or the 'I Am That I Am', this 'I' is Infinite and without bounds. On the other hand, the "i" that <u>thinks</u> it exists is limited by thought and is surrounded by a boundary called conceptual thinking or the universal mind."

"Putting this together, the universal mind is just a bundle of thoughts that thinks it exists. Not only does the universal mind think it exists, it thinks it can create other thoughts. It is because the universal mind thinks it has the power to create the universe as we know it, that we can also call the universal mind 'the creator god'. Actually the universal mind includes all the three mental gods that I will describe in more detail later, but I singled out the concept 'creator-god' because most people attribute an original creative force to a god. In Truth, this creative force is a thought of the universal mind."

"Now class, remember, these are just concepts I am talking about to explain the world that we think we know. They are symbols to help us conceptualize the invisible. The universal mind, functioning as the creator–god created time and space as its first act of creation. This act allowed all that appears to exist to come into existence. Without time and space, the universe as we know it, could not exist. Therefore, time became the basis from which we speak of a beginning and ending, or a past, present and future."

"Whoa, professor," interrupted Jamal. "You are getting deep – real deep. I am, like Carl, feeling somewhat uncomfortable with this theorizing, but it's fascinating. So, let me see if I can follow you. You're saying that there is or was an Existence, a Presence that had no form, and thus, was not manifested, at least not to human understanding. Then something seemed to occur like the Big Bang, and the universe appeared and simultaneously a world or existence of time and space came into being?"

"Excellent, Jamal," I exclaimed. "And once time and space were created, the world of form, which requires the principle of separation, came into being. This manifestation of the world of separate forms can parallel the Big Bang Theory or the Adam and Eve story in Genesis. Both theories require time and space, and both rely upon the premise of separation. It means one form or idea, is separate from another form or idea."

Carl seemed to be uncomfortable with my answer and raised his hand rather eagerly "So, is the Bible wrong, professor?"

Again, I knew I could easily be drawn into a religious debate that could never reach a definitive conclusion. So, I responded by saying, "I am not here to discuss anyone's religious beliefs or theology. Religion, for me, is a personal choice that one can make. If your religion gives answers to the ultimate question, then you should cling to your religion and its theological teachings. In this class, again, I remind you we are acting in the spirit of a liberal arts institution and inquiring into the nature of Truth. We are not assuming that we know what is true. We are only inquiring."

Carl seemed somewhat dissatisfied with my answer. I wanted to respect his beliefs. However, as a psychologist, I also wanted him to know the nature of the thought system called the mind. To accomplish that, Carl and the rest of us have to be willing to examine the possibility that everything we are aware of begins with a thought, and that thought is, or was, a thought of separation. That means one idea had to be separate from another. Carl nestled in his chair somewhat hesitantly as I continued with the lecture.

"When the world of separation and form was created, it obviously involved activity. The world of Presence or Being, which was before time and space, seemingly added the world of activity. In other words, the world of 'be' or 'presence' apparently had another dimension called 'do'. Action was taking place, and this action may have reflected what we call energy. One attribute of energy, as defined by scientists, is that it cannot be created or destroyed."

Jamal raised his hand and asked excitedly, "Is God therefore energy?"

A smile spread across my face as I absorbed Jamal's question. I knew he was beginning to go beyond the traditional way of thinking, which is always gratifying to any teacher dedicated to Truth seeking.

"I don't know," I replied. "All I can say about God, or at least the God that is beyond the concept that you and I were taught, is that It, She or He is beyond knowing. It is beyond thought, word, or concept. It is the Unknowable. Just be careful not to include that which is unknowable into what you already know, Jamal. That has been man's major failing, and has created almost all of his suffering and misery. If God is energy, then no one can know it. That is all I can say."

"Professor," said Jamal, "I will ponder that, but I hope you aren't coping out on me."

"Jamal, ultimately all is a cop-out because we cannot know all. We must get to a point where we can be comfortable with not knowing –to literally let not knowing be okay. I think it was Socrates who said: 'One thing I do know is that I don't know.' That is the beginning of wisdom."

I stood motionlessly as I encouraged Carl to continue with his questions.

"Does all this theorizing have any practical use for me when talking to my girlfriend, trying to pledge my fraternity, or dealing with my parents?" Carl continued.

"Those are important questions," I assured Carl. "I imagine they reflect some of your classmates' concerns. My point in this class is to show you that everything appears to begin in the mind, even time and space. Unless we know how the mind sets up everything in our lives from the thought of separation, we will never have any power with the mind. And, thus, we will be essentially powerless to fully understand or manage our everyday world.

The process begins with me. So, the 'I' that i think I am must be investigated. We must question psychology. We must ask if the profession of psychology is living up to its definition. We must ask if we are studying and understanding the essence of who we truly are.

"When we do this, we will see that the idea of separation from God or Infinity is what apparently started the world we live in. My purpose in this class and in life is to help you and me understand there is no separation from anything, that everything is connected and ultimately there is just One. Once we understand this, we will truly know the essence or soul of who we really are. Your first assignment is to start looking into your minds and observe your thoughts, feelings, and beliefs and see if you can discover anything that is the soul or essence of you. See you next week."

Chapter 4

From The One To The Many (The We-god)

As I was preparing my notes for the next class session, I realized the students and I had covered a lot of material in the prior lecture and the material piqued their curiosity. As an alumnus of Morehouse, and having grown up black, I was familiar with the backgrounds of my students. I knew the influence that religion played in their development, and the roles their parents and outside influences had in molding their values and beliefs.

I realized how important it was to be respectful of any position they might take in our classroom discussions. I knew fully well that as their professor, I was responsible for introducing them to new and scholarly ways to pursue Truth. With that thought in mind, I proceeded to finish my notes for the next lecture. I planned to address the role of environmental and social influences in understanding this thing called "I".

When class day arrived, I opened my lecture by giving the students an opportunity to talk about their homework assignment. Hands flew up immediately, as I encouraged them to participate in the discussion.

A student named Howard caught my attention. I acknowledged him.

"Professor, while doing the assignment, I noticed my thoughts never seem to stop. They just kept coming. Even when I tried to stop them, they would ask me why I wanted to try and stop them. And, no matter what, they just continued to come," Howard said.

"That's the nature of the mind," I told Howard. "You noticed a basic point, which is: the universal mind must produce thoughts. If you are observant, you can see how each thought is essentially seen as being separate."

Jamal was sitting next to Howard, and he was also eager to participate.

"Professor," Jamal intensely questioned, "are you saying that all matter, including Humans and non-humans, such as rocks, mosquitoes, and whatever, were made by the creator-god, which in actuality is not the real god?"

"The point I tried to make was that the universal mind, which is founded upon the principle of separation, apparently has a creative principle. I called this creative principle the creator-god. It seems to have power beyond human abilities. All created form, be they humans, rocks, mosquitoes or whatever, are symbolic of the principle of separation. They were created to substantiate the universal belief that all life, as we know it, depends upon separation and difference."

I paused after I made the assertion. I knew it added to the new and somewhat startling information the students had to process. I knew I was giving them a lot to deal with, but in my twenty-five-plus years of teaching at the college level, I had observed many times that students were able to grasp a lot of information even when it was radical or challenging to them. However, I was also aware that some students were more conservative than others, and those students had more difficulty accepting rather challenging ideas.

In particular, I was thinking of Carl. I knew he was a religious person who had a traditional view of God and God's creation of man. I saw Carl raise his hand.

"Professor, why do you use the term God to refer to these psychological concepts?" he asked. "I consider that to be offensive, and in my opinion, much of what you're saying hinges on being blasphemous." Carl was not angry, but was determined to get his point across.

I understood what he was saying, after all there was a time in my life when I would have thought what I was saying was offensive, even blasphemous. Therefore, I addressed his concern in what I hope was a sensitive fashion.

"I appreciate your honesty and understand your discomfort," I said to Carl. "But, you must remember that historically almost any of the advances in science that were not consistent with theological teachings were called blasphemous. My intention is not to offend you, but rather to push you to a point of inquiring. This may result in some uncomfortable feelings, and I apologize for that. Growth can be uncomfortable, and I believe what I am presenting can contribute to your intellectual growth. If it doesn't, then it surely can't hurt you, because you are strong enough to dismiss it as garbage if that's what you want to do.

So, please remember that I don't want to take anything away from you. I simply want you to ask questions, intelligent questions that can help free your mind."

"But," Carl replied, "Why do you have to use such names as creator-god, or whatever?"

I was grateful that Carl was asking these questions, and I could see he was at least struggling with the conditioning of his past. I was also appreciative that his questions provided an opening into my lecture.

"Do you recall the section in the Bible when Moses returned from the mountaintop and saw the Hebrews worshipping a golden calf god?" I asked.

"Sure", he quickly replied.

"Why do you think the Hebrews decided to worship a statute?" I asked.

"I assume they had a need to have something outside of them that they thought was more powerful than they were," Carl answered.

I smiled at Carl as I saw the reaction on his face. It was clear he was beginning to consider some new ideas.

"Exactly!" I exclaimed. "The universal mind cannot accept that it is all power because in Truth it is not. Only Infinity, or God, represents All Power. Thus, the mind must always say there is something external that has power, and one should submit to this power outside of oneself."

"This principle Carl, has been the nature of man since the beginning of time," I continued. "Man, in general, must have a god that is usually external to him, one that he believes is more powerful than he, a power he dares not question.

"Man does not see himself as possessing all-power. Thus, he must have an explanation for what he doesn't understand or control. Any thought which represents this idea . . . I will call a god. Man gives it his power, as in the case of the Hebrews and the golden calf.

"In Truth, we give our power away so frequently in our everyday lives that it is taken for granted. These false gods are, in reality, psychological beliefs that function in our lives mainly because we do not question them. Our unwillingness to question false beliefs gives the gods their power."

As the students pondered, I felt I had made a genuine connection with Carl. So, I continued my lecture by asking this question: "What is usually the first and the most impressive experience of power or authority to a young child?" I considered the question easy to answer, and those students that wanted to impress me quickly raised their hands. A chorus of voices answered the question before I could call on one person to answer.

"Our parents," the room echoed.

"Precisely, you all get an 'A'," I responded. They laughed half-heartedly as I proceeded with the lecture.

"Parents or guardians represent the most powerful figures to a child and thus, serve as models for god. They tell a child what to do, how to act, what to believe, and mold his or her values. In essence, they control almost all the child's activities and influence much of his thinking. Again, this underscores the basic principle of the creator-god. Parents are something separate from you, and this separate form has the power to control you.

"Consequently, this external power can dish out rewards or punishment. As the child matures, not only are parents seen as being powerful, but also other figures come into his or her life with similar authoritative functions. They may be teachers, relatives, preachers or whoever, but what they share in common is they are given positions of power over the child. The child's world is expanded to include many sources of authority, and these sources of authority I refer to as the we-god." (See illustration #2)

Another hand rose, it was Jamal who was eager to be recognized again.

"Professor, are you saying that the we-god is simply representative of those forces within our environment or society that mold and shape us into who we are?"

"Yes," I replied. "The we-god represents all the conditioning or teaching we receive from society about who we are."

Illustration #2

The Relationship Between Infinity, The Universal Mind, The Creator-god And The We-god.

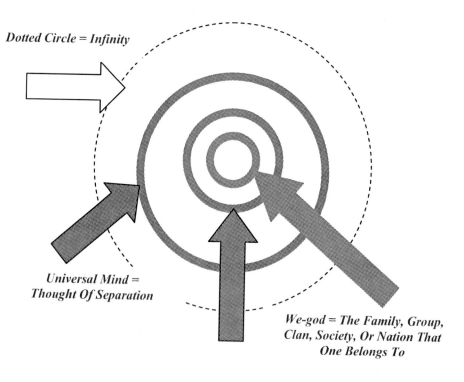

Dotted Circle = Infinity

Universal Mind =
Thought Of Separation

We-god = The Family, Group,
Clan, Society, Or Nation That
One Belongs To

Creator-god
(The Creative Principle)

I elaborated, "The we-god points out what is expected of us as individuals. It determines our values and requirements for group acceptance. It also deals with the consequences of violating group standards. The we-god also provides us with pictures of the way our lives are supposed to look.

"The creator-god and we-god are related because they have the same goal. They show you that separation is real and that real power resides outside of you and resides inside something or someone else," I replied. "Remember, the creator-god does not know of Infinity, but must create a seemingly infinite variety of forms to guarantee there is separation. Different varieties of forms are then separated into groups. These groups develop identities that are perpetuated by the we-god.

"The we-god offers us an acceptance, called belonging to a group. We now have group identity. We must conform to the group's standards if we want to be identified and accepted by it. Actually," I said to the class, "if you really knew and could see the mind, you would see that one of its primary functions is to create confusion so that Truth can never be recognized. Truth, however, must be consistent and clear, but the mind cannot understand that. So, it just creates confusion.

"If you are feeling confused," I added. "Just know that it is the mind that is responsible. So, just stay open-minded and continue to inquire. The mind cannot take too much inquiry. It definitely cannot stand openness and tolerance.

"Now, let me bring this idea or concept of the we-god home. The we-god can best be known through that old familiar phrase, *What would they say?* You know, the infamous 'they' that has a thousand faces. It's your mother, and it's your father. It's your grandmother, teacher, preacher, best friend, fraternity brother, boss and your lover. It's white people, black people, people of any race or gender. The we-god is everyone and everything that influences you, guides you, and sets expectations. You hear the voice of the we-god every minute of every hour.

"Carl, you brought up the issue of blasphemy earlier," I said. "Blasphemy is simply a judgment by a group that you have violated some of its highly valued beliefs. It is the we-god that proclaims that this is so."

"I don't think it is the we-god or a group standard," Carl interrupted. "I say it is God's standard that has been violated."

I asked Carl two questions, "Who told you that this is blasphemy? How do you know that I am violating God's Word?"

"The Bible told me," Carl answered.

"And where did you learn about the Bible?" I asked.

"At church and from my parents."

"So, it is reasonable to conclude that you were taught by others whom you respect? They probably told you that there is a code, or a belief system that you should not violate. Is that the case, Carl?" He remained silent for a few seconds and I knew I had to reassure him that my purpose was not to attack his faith or religious beliefs.

I therefore broke the silence by saying, "Carl, I respect your commitment to your religion and faith. I can see it is important to you and serves as a tremendous source of comfort and probably peace for you. That is good. Yet, we are here to look into the mind and see how it works. Clearly we see the mind is a belief system and as with any belief, be it religious, scientific or whatever, must be investigated, for the mind will at the very least distort it.

"It is the we-god that often serves as the source of many of our beliefs. Hence, we would be intellectually remiss if we did not look into this belief system called the mind. Once we determine how it works, we can keep any belief that we may have, because the mind must have beliefs.

"However, after you engage in this inquiry process, you will have at least opened your mind so you can expand your awareness." With that said, I asked Carl if he could agree on the value of the questioning process. A few seconds elapsed, but I could detect a change in Carl's expression, which began to reflect a degree of acceptance. Finally Carl said, "Sure professor. But, I hope a lightning bolt doesn't hit us."

I chuckled and said, "If it does, then I think I'm the only one who will be hit."

I then shifted my focus from Carl and addressed the entire class.

"I don't want you to think the we-god only deals with religion. In fact, let me ask, is there anyone in the class pledging a fraternity or who belongs to a fraternity?" A few hands went up and I called upon a student who identified himself as Joseph, who said he belonged to Alpha Phi Alpha.

"Good," I said to Joseph. "So do I. As you know, Joseph, Alpha men are expected to think a certain way and act a certain way. They are not to act like other fraternities such as the Kappas, Sigmas or Omegas. No, Alpha men act a certain way! Is that correct, Joseph?"

"Yeah, I guess so," replied Joseph. "And, everyone, especially the ladies, know that the Alphas are the greatest lovers."

Quickly a chorus of boos resounded, which I assumed came from the Kappas, Sigmas or Omegas. I hastily interrupted before a riot broke out and said, "Enough of the bravados. My point is that your fraternity or group has standards, expectations or norms, and if you violate them, you will suffer certain consequences. For example, Joseph, if you were to reveal the Alpha handshake to an Omega, you would probably receive some retribution from your fellow Alphas. Is that correct, Joseph?"

"Yes, that's for sure," he enthusiastically replied.

"Again," I said, "that is the we-god showing its presence. Another example that we are familiar with is when we hear such phrases as men are supposed to do this, or I wasn't raised to do such and such. That again is the voice and influence of the we-god. It is an authority that seemingly controls and dominates us. Powerful, right?" I heard a resounding yeah from the entire class.

"And how does it get its power?" I asked. Again Jamal's hand rose up quickly and he blurted out, "By using the old psychological principle of rewards and punishments."

"Yes," I said. "The we-god has the power to reward or punish its members in many ways, and it will do so even in aggressive and violent fashions, as history has shown us."

"Violate it and you will expect to pay a price," blurted Joseph.

"The voice and influence of the we-god, is an authority that seemingly controls and dominates us through rewards and punishments. Besides dishing out rewards and punishments, the we-god gains most of its power by convincing us that it is outside of us and has greater power than we do. That is its greatest trick, and the we-god does this in combination with the creator-god. Real power comes by questioning your seeming separation from the Infinite One. If you are separate from the Infinite, then the we-god and creator-god are powerful. If you are not then you can understand why Jesus told Pilate, 'unless your power comes from God, you have no power over me.' Do you think it is possible that 'me' cannot only refer to Jesus, but you and I? That remains to be seen, particularly as we look at the personal identity you call 'I' with your name attached to it. This will be the subject of our next class."

I dismissed the class wondering what they were departing with, but looked forward to our next lecture continuing our journey into this thing called I.

Chapter 5

The Personal Identity – The i-god

Prior to the next class, I was sitting in my office preparing the lecture knowing that this lecture would probably be the most important one, as the focus would be the personal identity – the "i" that you and "i" call ourselves.

I knew that this class would be particularly interesting because this is the "i" that is used when referring to our personal identity. It is this "i" we usually think of when we say "i", and it is this "i" that we think determines the world that we see and experience. Yet, it is this "i" that confuses us, and in fact limits us, from truly knowing who we are.

Thus, it was crucial that I prepared the lecture in a manner that opened my students to recognize what hinders them from knowing who they truly are. With all this in mind, I prepared my notes and was ready to proceed with the next day's lecture.

I began the lecture by asking the students what they meant when they used the word "I". A few hands went up, and I acknowledged Joseph.

"It is the personality, the self-concept, the way we view ourselves," Joseph said.

I asked him to define what he meant by personality.

"I'm not sure of the clinical definition," Joseph responded. "But, I think personality means the usual way we think and feel about ourselves."

The name of the course was Theories of Personality. So, I could not resist asking Joseph again what personality literally meant.

"Is there a catch or a hook?" Joseph asked somewhat cynically, not able to control his grin. "I could give you the book answer, but somehow or another, I think that is not what you are looking for. So, I give up. What is it?"

I told Joseph the term personality literally means mask. "We all know that a mask hides something, like on Halloween. So class, what we think we are is a mask that is hiding something."

"If what we think we are is a mask, and a mask conceals something, then what is it that our masks or personalities are concealing?" Jamal asked.

Somehow I knew Jamal would ask a question, because he didn't fear entering uncharted territory. "Class, the mask hides what you truly are by making you think you're something else. It makes you think you are a personal mind that is identified with a body that has a birth date and, of course, a death date."

"In between, you will use the body as the primary vehicle to have certain experiences, and to reinforce the idea that you are a human being separate from other beings. You think you are capable of being hurt, and vulnerable, and will always attempt to survive and get some degree of comfort and satisfaction. Out of the attempts to have these experiences you will have a personal story that to you, and others, will appear real. Then one day, you will die and some people may weep. Who knows what happens next? And so it goes with this story that the personal identity writes."

Instead of Jamal capturing my attention, Carl piped in.

"Professor," Carl interjected, "you make it sound so pessimistic, so cruel. Is that what life is about?"

"Unfortunately, Carl, human life is just what it is, and it may seem cruel. Big fish eat little fish, and so the story goes on. Life, as designed by the creator-god and we-god and experienced personally through the i-god, will always be a struggle. This is because the universal mind, with its three gods, is always incomplete. It is incomplete simply because only Infinity is complete and whole. The mind must show you a lack or loss and always indicate something is missing. As a result you, everyone and even me will always be motivated to get something. We will try to get something good, such as peace, happiness or even heaven. Or, we will try to avoid something that we view as negative, such as pain, injury, loss or hell. The bottom line is, we just can't have happiness or peace with the mind, Only God, or Infinity, can lead us to True Peace."

Carl and I connected. So did Jamal and a few other students in the classroom. Since I had their attention, I felt further explanation was needed to make sure they fully understood my points about the three gods and the universal mind (Illustration 3).

"There appears to be a creator-god and a we-god, and they seem to be outside of you. This is one of the greatest tricks of the mind. It makes you think there is a world outside of you but, in reality, there is nothing outside of you. You only think there is."

"Your mind is all that you know. It makes things appear to be outside of you when all you can Truthfully say is that you are only aware of what your thoughts inform you of. Even perceptions, what you feel, hear, and see, are essentially just thoughts or images that you are aware of. There is nothing outside of your awareness. You only think there is a world separate from and external to you, and you do so because the three mental gods dictate this belief."

Jamal finally broke in. "If you are talking about what I am aware of, then how come I don't know everything? How is it that I don't know the answers to my calculus test tomorrow, or better yet, even the winning lottery numbers for tomorrow, so that I can get rich, quit school and move to Tahiti?" he pondered, out loud.

"The answer is: you limit yourself to your personal identity and even at that, you limit yourself to only a small portion of your personal identity, like the tip of an iceberg. In other words, there are matters that you are unaware of. But, you can easily become aware of them, especially, in this day and age of the Internet. These things are in the subconscious mind. There is, however, a deeper level, which I will call the unconscious.

"In the unconscious things are so deeply imbedded and they cannot be easily assessed, but they are there (See Illustration #4). They represent that part of your mind that is the creator-god. They are the ideas and beliefs that all mankind have had since the beginning of time and space, when the very first thought of separation from Infinity seemingly occurred. This is within every mind, human or not, and connects us to all forms of matter that has ever been created. This is called the original creative principle and forms the basis of all creation in the universe. Because of this we are all really one, but since creation relies upon the belief in differences, we appear to be different. Indeed if we would just shift our identity from a personal one to that of the universal mind, we could be totally creative. The universal mind is the apparent source of creation and creativity. It is what has created all ideas and forms. But remember, it is not the Infinite One. It is the original covering that masks the Infinite One that may truly be called God."

"Wow," exhaled Jamal. "So at the most basic level in our unconscious minds, we are all the same?"

"Exactly," I exclaimed. "Our masks or personalities keep us from believing there is only One Infinite Mind by seemingly creating differences, such as a belief that there is a you and me who believe we are different personalities."

"Now, wait a minute," Carl interrupted. "I am different from you. I look different, maybe even better looking than you. Although you may be somewhat smarter than me, the point is that we are different. Now that is obvious. I don't need a Ph.D. to know this."

Yes, you are quite right, simply because your mind told you this Carl. If you will look a little deeper, you will see that not only does your mind tell you that you are different, but also that you are special. You said you were better looking than me. That may be debated, but the point "is, better than or lesser than comes from a principle of the mind

Illustration #3

The Relationship Between Infinity, The Universal Mind And Its Three Mental gods.

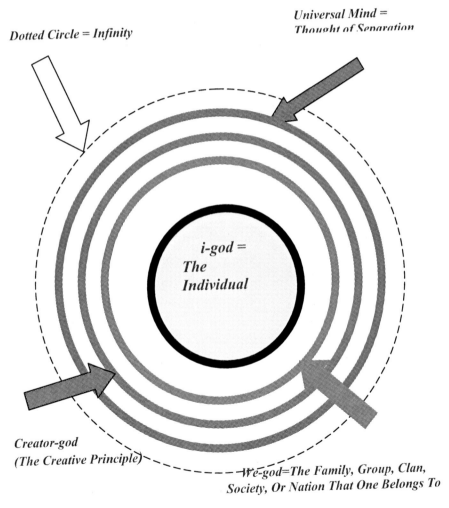

Universal Mind =
Thought of Separation

Dotted Circle = Infinity

i-god =
The
Individual

Creator-god
(The Creative Principle)

We-god=The Family, Group, Clan,
Society, Or Nation That One Belongs To

that says there has to be something or someone special. For instance, Carl, do you have a girlfriend?"

A smile quickly lit up his face and he beamed: "Yes professor, and she is quite lovely."

"Good, and she is special to you?"

"Yes, and she is mine," he beamed, grinning.

"Yes, I understand. You see, the mind has us caught in its story of separation and differences. It creates special people who we are to love and it even goes so far in some instances as to say that God has special people who He will accept into His home. This idea of special is so deeply rooted in our unconscious that it plays out through the we-god with our relationships, or through the i-god where we think that we have to be number one."

"We think we can possess or own something or someone. However, this is just one more example of the universal mind acted out by the three mental gods making us believe we are separate. They work together. The creator-god lays the foundation for separation, differences and special people and relationships. The we-god creates others, groups and institutions that use rewards and punishments to perpetuate the separation game. And, it is the human personality or i-god that experiences this world that is formulated in our unconscious. Remember, it is the unconscious or that which we are unaware of that seemingly rules us." Again I sensed confusion in the minds of some students, and Joseph's hand shot up.

"Professor, even if what you say is true, what's wrong with having separate identities if we are going to go to heaven?" he asked, looking perplexed.

"Even the idea you have of heaven, Joseph, is built on the principle of separation, differences, and special people or behaviors. We just can't get away from it - it is basic to human thought. This is not about right or wrong. This is simply a theory, a way of looking at the mind that may help you understand this crazy thing we call life."

"But is it necessary to know about the mind to understand life?" Carl asked.

"I really don't know, Carl. All I can say is: if you know your enemy, you have a better chance of defeating it. Get my drift?"

"Yes, I guess so," said Carl.

"But," injected Carl, "if this separation process is so important, why are you, a psychologist, so interested in it? Why do we as psychology students have to study this?"

"Because the separation process is fundamental to the basic component of the human mind. In our minds there is a core belief of the human personality that evolved from the creator-god and arose out of our unconscious. And that core belief is that we are inadequate and guilty (See Illustration #4). At the core of my personal identity, or anyone's personal identity, is a belief that not only am I inadequate, but I am also guilty. Every human, no matter how accomplished or successful he or she is, must feel inadequate because every human is inadequate. Only God or Infinity is adequate, complete and all-powerful. No human can be complete, or all-powerful. Hence, we feel not only incomplete and inadequate, but guilty."

"For example, let's review the Greek story of Prometheus. Prometheus stole fire from the gods and was afraid he would be punished. This mythical story actually says a lot about our human minds. Our minds would like to make us think we stole God's power by thinking we are independent and separate from Him, therefore, enabling us to think we have power that is not of God. As a result, we feel we have done something wrong, or sinned against God. In the biblical sense, we have disobeyed and sinned against Him. This is at the deepest level of our unconscious, and remains hidden in that part of our mind that we are unaware of (the unconscious).

"Every human mind has at its deepest core the belief that its owner is incomplete, inadequate, and guilty. At the deepest level we believe that we have committed the most unthinkable act. In other words, at the deepest level, we think we are absolutely evil – the devil incarnate, for we have stolen God's power. But, we dare not even look at this part of ourselves, so we either repress it, that is, keep it out of our awareness or we project it outside of us and call it the devil, the most horrible enemy there is.

"On a surface level or level of the personality, we experience the incompletion or inadequacy by believing that we are not good enough. And, we don't want anyone to know. But, the origin or basis of this feeling of inadequacy is the belief that we are not whole, that we are lacking or missing something. And, in Truth we are missing something.

At our very core we believe that we are un-whole or to say it another way, unholy or incomplete. We are incomplete because only Infinity is complete or whole. We feel as if we are missing something and are motivated to do something to cover up what is lacking or missing. We live our lives running away from lack, constantly motivated to get more, achieve some goal, or get to the top, believing we can become whole and others will see us as whole and adequate.

Yet, this is futile because we think we are human and can therefore never be whole, for only the Infinite One is whole, complete and perfect. Class, this is the core of the universal mind that appears to be the basis of all our identities!"

Carl and Joseph looked stunned. "Are you saying professor that there is no devil in hell?" Carl asked.

"Hell is simply an experience of no-love or where God isn't. It comes from a part of the mind that is definitely not loving – for this part of the mind thinks apart from Love or

God. It is the universal mind or ego. Often the term ego is used in spiritual and metaphysical literature to refer to the illusory belief that appears to be apart from the All that is.

"However, traditional psychology uses the term ego to generally refer to the personal identity or parts of the personality. Since there can be some confusion as to the definition and use of the term, it will be omitted in our discussions. Just know that spiritually speaking, the universal mind and ego are interchangeable."

"The universal mind, therefore, thinks it is separate from All – all things, all people, all forms – even the ultimate All – God. It does this simply by thinking it thinks. As a result of this belief, it not only feels guilty, but it remains in a constant state of fear. Since it knows not of love, it believes that fear is real. But, fear and perfect love cannot co-exist. Where one is, the other isn't."

Joseph interrupted and asked, "So are you saying the devil is just guilt and fear – just psychological attributes?"

My face beamed and I said, "If all that you know are your thoughts, which are psychological concepts, and if emotions such as fear and guilt are also psychological concepts, then the devil must also be a psychological concept or at the very least, a psychological experience. We experience the world through our thoughts, feelings and perceptions. These assertions, I know, may be somewhat startling to some of you, but they are assertions and this is a

Theory of Personality class. Theorists such as Freud, Jung, and Adler attempted to explain the mind, nothing more. Take what you can and leave the rest."

"But how are we able to function in our everyday lives if we are so evil, so sinful, so damned?" asked Joseph.

"The mind is very clever and attempts to survive. I've already mentioned the defenses of repression and projection. Repression keeps unwanted thoughts out of our awareness and projection places the negative outside of us. Remember the mind believes there is an internal world and an external world."

"But is that all the mind does that enables us to function, professor?" asked Joseph.

"No, the mind, as I said, is clever and it has many other defenses. It also loves to complicate life with what seems to be a complexity of events and happenings. Actually, the mind is quite simple. I've described the levels of the deepest parts of the unconscious, but on the more conscious level we have a core belief about ourselves that reflects a milder version of our feelings of inadequacy. All of us form our personalities around a core belief of inadequacy. Yet, this milder version can still be upsetting. So, we develop another strategy to deal with this feeling of inadequacy.

"We develop the looking good self. It is that part of us that knows how to win and achieve. It knows what the we-god wants and plays according to the rules. All of you know this part of yourselves. You are Morehouse men! You were probably academically successful in high school and knew how to present yourself to others as personable and intelligent young men. You know how to look and act the part. You know how to win! In fact, that is why you are here at Morehouse. That's the looking good self."

"But professor," interrupted Carl, "what's wrong with winning? What's wrong with being good?"

"Nothing," I said, "except it is not all of you. It is a façade – a covering for the inadequate part of you. One day you will discover, after being successful at whatever you do, that you will still feel empty and incomplete. You must because that core belief of inadequacy is still within you, only hidden at times by the looking good self.

Eventually, one day you will look in the mirror and wonder who you are and why you are not happy, despite your achievements or accomplishments. When that happens, you may really begin an earnest process of asking, who am I?"

"Professor, if we have this core belief of inadequacy and if it can show up for us differently, as molded by our personalities, how can we recognize it?" Jamal broke in, and shifted the discussion somewhat.

"Jamal, this core belief acts like a railroad track. It runs our lives. All we need to do is look at the patterns in our lives and we will see the unique form that have this core belief of inadequacy has taken for us. Our lives are not random accidents. Our three mental gods program them, and they have a pattern. Just discover your pattern and you will know your particular core belief. More practically, you will probably see it revealed in your pattern of personal relationships, as these relationships usually reveal the more intimate parts of ourselves."

"Professor, are you talking about love relationships as in the boy and girl thing?" asked Joseph.

"Joseph, are you in love?"

"Yes, in fact, we plan to get married as soon as she finishes Spelman College."

"Good and I'm happy for you, but remember, the odds against marriages succeeding are in the negative. Less than fifty percent of all first marriages make it without going to divorce court, because the mind does not want you to be happy. Remember, I said at all levels of the mind, at the creator-god level, the we-god level, and the i-god level, we feel inadequate and afraid. And, we bring these feelings into our love relationships looking for love and hoping that the other will make us happy. Rarely is that accomplished. Our true happiness can only come from within and not from the parts of the mind that I have identified.

"There is another part of the mind that I have not mentioned that is present within all of us. In fact, when the universal mind formed the concept of separation and hence creation, a part of the mind that knows of Truth was also implanted in our minds. That part of the mind that is ever present but hidden by the mask of personality is the Higher-Self. It is that part of us that knows Truth. It is that part of us that knows of Truth. It is all-powerful and able to love unconditionally.

It knows that we think we are separate from God and also knows the way back home – the way back to heaven. It is not a thing or a thought for it cannot be confined or defined by thought. It just is! It is there always and can be known to us if we are quiet enough to still the voices of the three little mental gods. It is the true us! It is the one that I think Jesus referred to when he knew his true identity was not a personal one or one attached to a body/mind form. He knew his identity was spiritual and thus, he was able to say, 'I and the Father are One'. Not the I that has a thought of separation, guilt or fear, but an I that is Infinite, that is complete, that is whole, that is All love.

That 'I' is beyond psychology, it just is. It is the 'I Am that I Am'. It is the only I. It is the I that is All, and it is not a personality. It is you. It is all of us because It is One. There is no other, no separation, ultimately no human thought. One day we will know we are not separate from each other or from God. This is something the mind cannot grasp, because psychology as presently structured, is not focused on the essence of who you or I are. Yet by definition, psychology is the study of the soul. And to know the soul, we must get behind the mask, behind the personality and see the only Truth there is. We must understand that there is only one I and that I is the 'I Am That I Am'. Class dismissed."

Chapter 6

More On The Universal Mind And The i-god

As the class exited from the room, I detected a great deal of concern and dismay. It was as if I had pulled a rug from underneath their feet. I knew this could leave them feeling vulnerable and even threatened. Yet, as this feeling emerged, I could not help but reflect on a saying by Lao Tzu, the founder of Taoism, "A true teacher is out to destroy you." Wow! What an assertion. Sounds cruel and even violent on the face of it, but when one really ponders the "you" that is to be destroyed, then, a different picture can emerge. The you that must be destroyed is the personal "i" – the mask that hides the true essence of what you are. This is the task of a true teacher. The Truth will emerge when that which is false disappears. With this in mind I returned to my office and prepared the notes for the next class period to continue with the exposure of the lie and unveil the mask that attempts to cover the Truth of our identity.

When the next class period arrived, I was not surprised to have the first question come from Carl.

"Professor, I was thinking about the last few lectures where you described the scene when Jesus stood before Pontius Pilate and stated that Pontius Pilate had no power over Jesus. Do you recall that?"

"Yes, I do Carl."

"Well, I can accept that part of your statement that referred to Jesus, because we know Jesus is the Messiah and The Son of God, but you really shocked me when you said that "we", meaning you or "i", could also make that statement to any Pontius Pilate in our lives. That sir, I think is heresy, and it upsets me because you seem to be equating yourself with Jesus and that is totally ridiculous and blasphemous. If you were equal to Jesus, then why don't you walk on water or change water into wine? Can you do that professor?"

I smiled as he asked this question for I sensed that Carl was really struggling with the ideas presented in class, and I really appreciated his struggle.

"Carl, it is crucial that you understand what I am talking about when I say 'I' or 'me' or 'you'. As humans, we have only one problem, and that problem is that we are misidentified. We have a mistaken identity and from this mistaken identity all of our problems, limitations, worries, disappointments and troubles surface. That mistaken identity is believing that we are a human identity. We think this personality is a belief system enclosed in a body born of a woman and destined to die. This primary belief is the basis of all human identities and forms the ground-work for the human personality as dictated by the i-god.

"Jesus must have known the distinction between his personal identity as Jesus and his identification as the Christ. Otherwise, how could he have made such statements as: 'Of myself I can do nothing but it is the Father within that does the work.' The 'of myself' referred to his personal identity as Jesus the human. This is the part of Him we can relate to since we think we are human identities. But note, He was saying the human identity is impotent – it can do nothing. Only the Father within or God, Omnipotence or Infinite Being can ,do or have any power.

"Yet, Jesus is also credited with saying 'I and the Father are One' and 'I Am The Way, The Truth and The Light.' All of these sayings show His identification as the Christ, which is unconditional love or reflects the Higher Self (See illustration #4). Some people may call it the Holy Spirit or Higher Consciousness. Regardless of the name, the main point to remember is there is a Presence that is unconditional love and is everywhere (Omnipresent) and all powerful (Omnipotent). This Presence is seemingly covered by the universal mind."

Jamal broke in, "Professor, I think I feel kinda like Carl. What you are saying may or may not be blasphemous, but it is making me uncomfortable."

I knew that I had to settle the class down and make my point as clearly as possible.

"Jamal, I appreciate your honesty and concern. As humans, our only concern is the issue of identity. It is central to all existence, all conversations, all beliefs, all disciplines and all theologies, because what you believe you are will determine how you perceive the world. Remember, I said there appears to be a personal identity that is connected to a form and we call that identity our personality. This identity is usually the focus of traditional psychology. This identity is what most of the world thinks is the core of their existence. Yet, I maintain, this psychological based identity is, as Jesus said, impotent and powerless."

"Our Spiritual identity is the only identity that has power. It is omnipresent, everywhere present, nowhere absent, and hence, is here now. But, we don't identify with it. We think we are not It. We think we are humans, and we cover up our true identity with a mask called personality. Jesus, however, knew His identity was not psychological, but Spiritual. It was invisible, omnipresent and not separate from God. This Spiritual identity cannot be equated with human identity. Our physical bodies are not Christ. There is, however, that which is omnipresent, everywhere present, nowhere absent, which is our Real and True Identity. That is what we must see and come to know. It is so important for you to know, to truly know, the difference between that which you think you are and that which you truly are. Now, am I coming across clearly?"

"Yes, I guess so, but if I am Christ, how come I don't know or act like it?"

"The reason we don't, Jamal, is we listen to the dictates of the universal mind with its three mental gods. We think and because we think, we believe that we are psychological beings operating in a physical world. Actually, everything we see or think about is really all mental – all thoughts that appear to take form. It is really just a mental game."

"Now, wait a minute," screamed Joseph. "This has gone far enough! Are you saying that this world is all mental? To me that sounds crazy and, pardon me professor for saying this, but I don't know if you took your medicine this morning."

I grinned as Joseph commented. I knew I may have gone too far, but I believed if I was sensitive to their feelings, I could take them to a new and expanded place.

"Joseph, have you ever heard an athlete say that a game is 90% mental and 10% physical?"

"Yes," replied Joseph. "But, if a big 250 pound linebacker is coming at you wanting to knock your head off, Buddy, that is not mental. That is pure physical."

"Yes, I know the pain will be felt but it is important to remember that even the athlete is recognizing the primary importance of the mental component. And again, I would ask, how would you know you were in pain if it were not for your mind? Your mind tells you what is painful or not. There are Tibetan Monks who can sit in the Himalayan Mountains overnight in snow and not get frost bitten and can melt the snow around them by meditating – getting to a higher state of consciousness in the mind. For instance Joseph, can you recall your dream from last night? Did the characters appear real to you?"

"Of course they did."

"Did you respond to them as if they were real?"

"Sure did, and it was nice!"

"Okay Joseph, we won't ask her name or what you did, but, the point is, did the dream seem real to you while you were dreaming?"

"Yes."

"Good. Now what told you it was real while you were dreaming?"

"I don't know. I guess it was my mind. What else?"

"Yes, it had to be your mind. Then you woke up, right? And, what told you that you were awake?"

"I guess it was my mind."

"Exactly, it is always your mind. It tells you that you are awake and it tells you that you are dreaming. But, who knows what we are experiencing now? Are we dreaming; yet, the mind says we are awake? When you were dreaming, your mind made it seem real. When you are awake, your mind makes it seem real. So, who is to know?"

"But professor," Carl interrupted, not being able to hold off any longer. "All of us, Joseph, Jamal and the rest of the class can verify that this is real, and we are awake."

"Good point, Carl. But in your dream, aren't the others verifying that the actions of the dream are real?"

A silence came over the room. I let this sink in for a while.

"The Truth is that we don't know what is real other than existence exists or Infinity is. It is only the mind that makes us think we know what is real and true and this mind cannot be relied upon for it does not know of Truth or Infinite Awareness. It is therefore very crucial that we question the mind and see it for what it really is – a deceiver and a liar –

always afraid that it will be exposed as being a mask that conceals."

"Professor, since this is a Theory of Personality class, haven't other people such as Freud, Adler, Skinner, and Jung addressed this issue?" Carl asked, raising his hand. "What makes you think that you are special and are saying something that they didn't?" Carl continued.

"Carl, I'm not special. Indeed the mind loves to think it is special and has special or important ideas. My thoughts are not new, special or important. They are only thoughts about the thought machine, the mind. All of the theories from Freud to Skinner are worthwhile theories for their purpose, but they all begin with the premise that there is a human personality and this premise is never questioned."

"My approach, on the other hand, says there is only Infinity or Omnipresence and this Infinite One cannot be known by any thinking, limited, conceptually bound mechanism called the human mind. To think that we can know anything is pure arrogance! Only Infinite Intelligence or Omniscience can know! But we perpetuate a dream world that thinks human personalities are real and true. We don't see that there cannot be an All-knowing Infinite One and something else that thinks it knows also. We believe we exist as individual personalities. We can't accept the fact that only GOD or Infinity is All, PERIOD! We disavow this premise because accepting it would mean the death of the human mind.

Lao Tzu said a true teacher was out to destroy you. Jesus said of himself he could do nothing. We must always be aware of this and stay with what is true, real, love or God. Yet, the mind won't let us do this because its basic premise is that we are not love but are guilt and fear based. Carl Jung attempted to approach this dilemma with his theory but he made the mistake of so many theorists. He began his theory with the premise that the human mind exists and it can be self actualized."

"What's wrong with self actualization? To me it's like realizing that we can go to heaven," Carl eagerly said.

"There is nothing wrong with it per say, Carl. But it makes the error real – that there is a man and that man can become something else, even actualized! In Truth, there can only be the Infinite One and that One is All. The river must flow into the ocean and become the ocean. There cannot be Infinity and its opposite – finiteness. The river cannot be part of the ocean. The ocean consumes the river; hence, there is only ocean. There is only room for one in heaven and that one is God or Love or Infinite Being. In Truth, there is no personal I or personal you. There cannot be any forms as perceived by humans, for forms, by definition, are limited, thereby seemingly making real that which is impossible – the opposite of Infinity or God."

"Hold your horses, professor. Are you saying that I or my good God-fearing and praying grandmother can't go to heaven?"

"Who knows for sure, Joseph? All I'm saying is that Infinity cannot have an opposite, and we must use Infinity as our basis of any inquiry if we want to know Truth. Anything else is just making the dream or error seem real."

"So do we just throw out all the psychological and theological theories and dump them in the trash can as worthless?" Carl asked.

"Carl, I'm not here to tell you what to do. In fact, it would be impossible for you or me to give up our psychological beliefs easily, for the dream seems so real. We can still use these theories to help us understand. In fact, I think Jung's ideas of the collective unconscious and archetypes support the concept of the universal mind and its three gods, because Jung points to a part of our minds that connects us to everything and everyone from the beginning of time. All things, events and circumstances can be traced back to the beginning of time and the universal mind with its three gods.

"Indeed, the world that we think exists is just a dream that is a projection of the universal mind. The function of the universal mind and its three mental gods is to keep the dream alive and seemingly real. Basic to this dream is the idea that there are separate forms that have independent power to do things that may be labeled bad or good. From this act of judgment, stories evolve that create the adventure of what we call life. It is the belief that we have creative power that pushes us to do and seemingly accomplish things.

"So therefore class, go out into your world. Do whatever you think you can choose to do, and do it with vigor and determination. Create, act, accomplish, achieve. Do it! In fact, you can create beyond your wildest dreams, because of the seemingly creative power of the universal mind. But remember, always remember that maybe it isn't you that is doing it. Maybe there is an Infinite Power that you have not explored yet that can know all, do all, and be all because it is All. It is Omnipresent. And this identity I say is the true you, the true me, the true Self that I Am. I'll see you in the dream. Class dismissed."

PART II

THE TEN COMMANDMENTS OF THE THREE MENTAL GODS

Chapter 7

Introduction of the Commandments of The Three Mental Gods

As a psychology professor and as a psychotherapist, I am aware of the importance of understanding the mechanism that runs and ruins our lives. That mechanism is the mind. It's not the mind that you and I ordinarily think of.

I am referring to the universal mind, the original thought of separation. The universal mind created the beliefs that we use to structure a world where we are the central character interacting with other beings.

This universal mind establishes the belief that this is the real world, a world built upon an individual, personal identity that apparently has private thoughts. Those thoughts are separate and unknown to other personal identities that also apparently have private thoughts. There appears to be a world that is internal to me, and a second world that is external, or rather, outside of me. I therefore, have a personal identity that is separate and apart from other identities. As a result, I have a personality, a mask that I call "I." It must believe it is separate from all other identities, forms and ideas. To further the principle of separation, the universal mind constructs three primary functions that I refer to as mental gods.

This term is used loosely because the mental gods appear to be so powerful, and seemingly, are so unquestionably real, that they serve god-like functions in our lives. The term god usually refers to a concept of a source of power, love, comfort, protection, and in some cases, self-esteem. These three gods: the creator-god, the we-god and the i-god, like many god-like figures, must have rules and laws.

Indeed, one of the ways they maintain their god-like status is to create a sense of order, in an effort to prevent us from experiencing what we would call chaos. We believe they will reward us if we follow their rules and punish us if we do not; this reward or punishment creates order.

Similar to Moses going to Mount Sinai for the Ten Commandments, the universal mind gives each of the three mental gods ten commandments that require absolute submission. These laws and rules structure our world and give us experiences in what we assume to be our reality and identity. It is therefore vital that we examine and understand these commandments if we are to know who we really are or understand this thing called "I".

In the following pages, you will find Ten Commandments for each mental god. Each will be explored, with examples to illustrate how they lock us in our psychological prisons. Following this section, we will examine ways to escape from the mental prisons that seemingly incarcerate us. So, let's begin this voyage within the inner recesses of our minds and discover all the laws and rules that we have been given to deceive us into thinking we are not love, not beautiful, not whole, not competent or not adequate.

We must discover what keeps us from knowing our true identity. For if we don't know and understand what is running and/or ruining our lives, we have little hope of changing our conditions or ourselves. With this understanding, let's proceed on our adventure.

Chapter 8

The Ten Commandments of the Creator-God

The Ten Commandments of The Creator-God

I. You will have no awareness, knowledge or understanding of Infinity.

II. You will believe that thought is power.

III. You will believe that not one but two or more is the basis of life.

IV. You will believe that one must have an opposite.

V. You will believe that you are guilty because you think you are separate from God.

VI. You will believe that each living form struggles for survival and fears its own non-survival.

VII. You will believe that all human form has lack and loss as key components of its identity.

VIII. You will believe that all human form must have a cause and each cause must have an effect.

IX. You will believe that life has a purpose.

X. You will believe that each human form has free will and free choice.

The Creator God

I. Commandment

You will have no awareness, knowledge or understanding of Infinity.

Webster defines Infinity as: without boundaries and limits, immeasurably great. How can you truly understand or comprehend words such as without boundaries, or immeasurable? How can I, a personal mind that uses concepts to understand my world, understand that which is beyond concept? How is that possible? If it were possible, then either Infinity would have to shrink so it can be put into a container called concept, or Infinity would have to blow apart all concepts that you or I have.

I recall attending a spiritual class and listening to a speaker describing God as an Infinite Being or Consciousness. The words sounded nice, but I couldn't make them real. At some level I knew the point the speaker was trying to make, but it seemed a little too abstract, a bit over my head, not real. Yet as I began to let it sink in, I eventually reached the conclusion that Infinity can only Be. It cannot be obtained by my puny little concepts, which try to categorize the unknown into familiar and known concepts. This little mind of mine, which struggles to understand the world, cannot understand or fully grasp that which is beyond knowing, that which is beyond any concept, familiar or unfamiliar.

Naturally, I was not comfortable with the idea that there is something that I cannot know or understand because it limits me and makes me feel powerless, even somewhat stupid. I realized I had to let go of wanting to fully understand and know that which is unknowable – that which is Infinite. Once I was able to settle into this position, I was able to see that the idea of a creator-god is only natural. I can understand the concept of a creator. I am a parent, and I can comprehend the idea and role of a father figure who is the source of life, love, and protection. The concept became comfortable and easy for me to grasp.

As a father of two sons, I participated in a creation process and live as a protector, a provider, and a source of love for them. The concept of this type of god is one that, as the old folks say, "Sits down easy with me." The Infinite has now become finite. The Infinite is now a concept limited to a category called thought, and all thoughts are limited. No thought, not even Infinity, is unlimited because it is a thought in the service of the mind. But my mind, especially the part that is spiritual, quickly conjures another thought: "Are you saying that there is no god or that god is limited?" The answer is, there is always Infinity, but I as a limited, concept bound, human thinking mind can never grasp, know of, or even approach understanding It. It, God or Infinity just IS and whether I understand or fully grasp It is irrelevant. In fact, It was, is and always will be, regardless of my limited understanding. So, let's see what else there is to this creator-god that knows nothing of Infinity.

The Creator God

II. Commandment

You will believe that thought is power.

It's Rene Descartes, the famous philosopher, mathematician, and scientist, who is famous for saying, "I think, therefore I am." This often quoted statement has baffled many theologians and philosophers, but it is the basis of the creator-god. It is thought that serves as the basis of all human life. For without thought what would you be? How would you know about it? It is thinking that serves as the vehicle of awareness for human kind. Just think about it. Oops, I'm sorry! Don't think about it. Just don't think. Okay? Just be, okay? What are you doing? Are you thinking? Well, let's see, let me think about it or not think about it.

Seems as if we are caught up in our thoughts. And it is this thinking process that gives rise to all creation. All things, whatever form they may take, were originally thoughts. Before anything took form, it was a thought in someone's mind. The chair you are sitting in was the thought of a furniture maker. The book you are reading was a thought in my mind. Thoughts, therefore, appear to have power because they seem to be the basis of everything and from which everything arises.

How else would you or I know about them? To be sure some people, especially psychologists, may say that activities can occur on an unconscious basis, but that is still a thought. Any idea, be it unconscious, conscious, instinct or intuition, is at the most basic level just a thought.

This idea that everything is just a thought was initially unsettling. Surely, this desk before me is not just a thought. I know it is not. I can touch it. I can see it and hear it creaking. I know it is real and thus, cannot be just a thought. True, it appears outside of my mind, but another part of me says, 'I wouldn't know it is outside of my mind or know that I could touch, see, or hear it creaking, if I were not aware of this information.' And, the only way I can be aware of this information is to think about it – to have ideas of it. God! It was so uncomfortable thinking of it that way, but again, I was just thinking thoughts.

Was Descartes right? Yes and no! He was right to the extent that the creator-god creates this world with thought, but he was wrong in the sense that the first commandment states that there is a reality beyond thought that the human mind knows not of and cannot think of. This reality, which is beyond thinking, is the true reality of my identity. I am not what I think.

The true power of who I am is in the world of the Infinite or as Jesus Christ stated, "My kingdom is a world ye know not of." That world is beyond thought because it is Infinite and

Eternal. The world of the creator-god – the world you and I are familiar with - is a world that is defined and confined by thoughts, which appear to have power and to be real. But, that which is real is beyond thought – beyond the world that was made by the creator-god. So, what else does the creator-god command to keep us unaware of the Infinite?

The Creator God

III. Commandment

You will believe that not one but two or more is the basis of life.

Once there is thought and it appears to have power, each one must have as its basis the perception of differences. One thought has to be different from another. Otherwise, they would be the same. And, that would mean everything would be the same. This cannot be because I know that there are differences. I can see, hear, taste, and smell differences. I know that to be true.

This commandment thus seems to be simple, but once I began to consider it, I also realized this commandment has profound implications. Several questions arose in my mind. What would the world be like if there were no differences? What if this was not separate from that? I then realized that if there were no differences, there would be no separation. If there were no separation, everything would be the same. What if everything was the same? The mind would literally fall apart. The mind has to have differences. In fact, if it did not have differences it would not know what to do. It could not think. It could not even help us speak.

All words are founded on the premise that each word has at least one essential quality that makes it different from other words. Words insure the basic premise that separation and differences are at the very core of this world we live in. For example, I have an idea in my mind but I think you do not know what it is. So, I speak some words to you that I think you understand, since we speak the same language. You now know what I was thinking about.

Basic to this interaction is the premise that there are differences and separation. I think I am separate from you and have something that you don't have – my ideas. My ideas are, thoughts, separate from you, although through the conversation I am attempting to lessen the separation that appears to exist. I am attempting a communication process – a union of two separate and different forms. When that communication actually occurs and the separation and differences are lessened, true joining occurs. True communication begins.

I can recall a time when I was attempting to get a friend to understand my point. It seemed as if we were poles apart and on the verge of arguing. But, as I lessened my need to make my point and saw what his position was, I noted the commonality between our positions. We actually began to communicate. We had joined. The two separate positions ceased to be and communication had occurred. If we think about it, the purpose of all communication is to unify at least two separate and different positions.

To take that a step further, when two join, they become one and once there is one, there is love. True communication is therefore a form of lovemaking. But, this process goes against the commandment of the creator-god, which attempts to ensure that true communication does not occur and maintains the premise of, two or more. To make certain that there are two or more, the creator-god takes another step and gives the following commandment.

The Creator God

IV. Commandment

You will believe that one must have an opposite.

In the book of Genesis, in the Bible, the story is told of God planting a tree in the Garden of Eden that represents the knowledge of good and evil. Adam and Eve were commanded not to eat of the fruit of the tree. When they disobeyed God's commandment they left the garden with the knowledge of good and evil, and were forced to struggle for their survival.

This story was always fascinating to me, because it gave an account of the origin and nature of man's existence. I know that Adam and Eve not only disobeyed God, they also acquired the knowledge of good and evil. They now knew that there were opposites - that good had an opposite called evil. And, once Adam and Eve had this knowledge they were no longer in the Garden of Eden.

This made sense to me. Life does appear to be about the play of opposites. Good does appear to have an opposite called evil. Up has an opposite called down. Negative is in opposition with positive and we all know women and men are opposites in so many ways. Life is a play of opposites and what a play it is. In fact, it seems as if all human drama is built around the theme that opposing forces must compete with each other. Just look around you. Pick up the daily newspapers. The majority of the stories discuss one party or individual, against another. Republicans against Democrats, blacks against whites, men against women. In fact, when I examine my life, I can see that it is just a long story of struggles against opposing forces. As a Black man, I see White people as opposites. As a heterosexual, I see homosexuals as different and opposites. But probably most basic to my story is the premise that I, as a man, see women as opposites. And, viva la difference!

But this opposite of me creates the energizing forces of my life story. It is what keeps the story of my life going and if you are Truthful, you may see a similar theme in your life. The play of opposites is the very fuel or gasoline that runs this life story, and it all can be traced to the belief that one has an opposite – something that is not only different but, as defined by Webster, is directly contrary in nature or kind. Good is indeed directly contrary to evil. God is definitely not the devil. The devil is His opposite and surely is contrary to the nature and awareness of God. I have been taught this from the early teachings of my grandmother and mother. In my Sunday school classes, I was taught that God and the devil are not the same. They are opposites.

To challenge such a belief to me seemed blasphemous. Even when I began to think that it might be possible that God and the devil were not opposites, I would shudder. Yet, if there is only one Infinite presence, if there is only one Infinite intelligence, called Omniscience, Omnipotence, and Omnipresence, how can there be an opposite? Can Omnipresence also have an opposite that resides in a place where God is not? This idea made me tremble, and even run. Initially, I could not consider it, but as I reminded myself of my journey to seek Truth, I had to reconsider all the teachings of those whom I loved and respected. The Truth is, only Infinity exists and It is All there is. The struggle seemed so intense then. Later I realized the struggle was simply my unwillingness to let go of the commandments of the creator-god, which were "two or more must exist" and "these two or more have to engage in a play of opposites that create the human story that we call life."

With this knowledge, I was able to let the human story play out as the creator-god would have it do, but hold on to the knowledge that behind this human story is that which is unknown, unthinkable, unseen. It is the invisible presence of Spirit that remains true for all eternity. It is the Kingdom that Jesus described where "the sheep shall lie down with the lions" and all men and women know no differences or opposition. But this is not the world of the creator-god. This is not the world that you and I experience. So, what is the world that we experience?

The Creator God

V. Commandment

You will believe that you are guilty because you think you are separate from God.

Let's return to the story of Adam and Eve as depicted in Genesis. Central to the story is God commanding Adam and Eve not to eat the fruit of the Tree of Knowledge. Upon discovering that they had disobeyed Him, God judged them as guilty and Adam and Eve either left the garden or were thrown out, depending on which version of the Bible you believe.

I remember reading this story at a young age in Sunday school, and recall being taught that Adam and Eve had sinned and were indeed guilty. I thought at that time that I too could also sin and be judged by authorities, be it my parents, teachers, preacher or whomever. Guilt was introduced in the human world by Adam and Eve and introduced into my life by my parents and others. My life from then on was a never ending battle with and avoidance of this treacherous monster called guilt. Almost every story that we can think of includes the element of guilt.

Someone has done something wrong and has been judged by another and therefore, must be punished. Every day the soap operas portray individuals as good or bad guys. Not only is this the meat of soap operas, it is the very fuel that runs our lives. I need not recall the many punishments I received as a child for doing the wrong thing. I was a smart aleck but basically a good kid. As I reached adolescence, I quickly knew about guilt because I was aware of sex. One can't be raised in this society, taught about sex and not know about guilt. I hope my point is obvious. Guilt plays a powerful role in our lives.

Seemingly forgotten in this knowledge is the origin of guilt. The story of Adam and Eve states God proclaimed them guilty. God was the judge who decided something had gone wrong. Guilt therefore, always requires a judge and, that which the judge does best, judging. But in the Adam and Eve story, where did God get the idea that he could judge another?

Clearly, God must have thought he was not Infinite and All. Otherwise there wouldn't be any one else to judge. The god, therefore, of which we speak must be the creator-god. That means he is not Infinite but has limits and boundaries. He knows of others that are not him, which he thinks he created.

By being the creator, he is not aware of his Infinite nature or anything not created by him. One of his most important acts is to judge others as guilty or not guilty, blessed or damned. From this first act of judging, all other acts of judging have ensued. And by virtue of being the off spring of the creator, and made in his image, we also judge others as guilty. The story goes on and on: Adam judged Eve as guilty, Eve judged the serpent as guilty and the serpent is left to his evil ways.

I realize that what I have said may be unsettling to some of you, but I ask you to consider the possibility that Infinity cannot judge or declare anyone guilty because Infinity is complete onto Itself and knows not of opposites or anything apart from It. Therefore, are you guilty? Only in the human drama, created by the creator-god is this question relevant. Only if the creator-god knew Truth would this be irrelevant. Then and only then.

Infinite, which is unconditional love, knows of no condition that can be violated or commandment that can be disobeyed. Unconditional love is just that, unconditional. No judgment is ever made! I think that was the purpose of the story of the prodigal son. It depicted a father who was unconcerned with the acts of his child, and only wanted him to return home. This unconditional love is not comprehendible by the human mind. It is a threat to the creator-god who constantly weaves a story of human suffering and pain built upon guilt. However, guilt alone is not a powerful enough force for the creator-god. It must have another force of equal power to render man submissive to its commandments. So, let's see what that force is.

The Creator God

VI. Commandment

You will believe that each living form struggles for survival and fears its own non-survival.

Growing up in a Christian home, I was taught that it was a virtue to fear God. Although this was my instruction, I was confused by this message. I didn't understand why I should fear God, a God who was portrayed as love. I remained confused as I listened to the elders of my community talk of judgment day and how God would have people account for their sins, and if found guilty they would be condemned to hell. This story of being sent to hell for all eternity was intended to evoke fear, and I suppose it did for a time. But, there remained a restless part of me that just could not reconcile the God of all love that Jesus spoke of and a god that I was supposed to fear.

As a psychologist, I often see patients who are paralyzed by fear. Recently I counseled a client diagnosed with paranoia whose life was literally dictated by fear. He was constantly afraid someone would hurt him or perpetuate some untold threatening act. Yet, paranoids are not the only ones whose lives are controlled by fear. Freud said that anxiety is the key component of the human mind and a basic component of anxiety is fear. So fear is present in our lives. And, the fear that is universal to man is the fear of death.

I can recall a time I had a close call with death as a child. My experience happened while swimming with the Boy Scouts. I swam past the safety zone and got caught in a strong current. I remember struggling, gasping for air, and begging God to help me. I was terrified and really thought I was going to die. When I finally made it to shore, I was filled with relief. I quickly thanked God and vowed to read my Bible daily.

The question that constantly plagued me was, if we are all going to die, why fear it? And herein the creator-god steps in and brings the powerful forces of guilt and fear. Most of us, particularly in the West, were probably taught that if we didn't act in accordance with God's wishes we would die and spend eternity in hell. The fear of God was coupled with our guilty acts. God was thought of as a punishing God, because He judges. And once He judged a person wrong, a punishment followed. Guilt always demands punishment in the mind of the creator-god.

God could therefore be viewed as a wielder of punishment for bad deeds or as a giver of blessings for good deeds. Always lurking in my mind was the idea that God was to be feared, especially since I didn't know when or under what condition He would strike.

When we were children, my sister would say that God knew every bad thing that I had done to her, and He or daddy would "get me" and make me pay. To some extent I actually believed it, although it did little to alter the way I treated my sister. But the point remains: God and fear were tied together more often than God and love. In fact, some psychologists think the more a child associates an authority figure with fear, the more fearful his/her God is.

Therefore, fear is tied to God and God to death. Death is usually perceived as death of the body. But can this be questioned? Before you dash off and call the boys in white coats on me, I must say I know the body dies. It comes into this existence and goes through the aging process, the process we call being born, living, aging, and then dying. This is the way of all living Beings. But, is it the only form of death?

Since by now you should know that we are asking the forbidden and thinking the unthinkable, I would ask you to consider a deeper or more profound fear even beyond the fear of the extinction of the body. Ponder the extinction of the mind. In fact, the mind is not afraid of losing the body. This was so aptly illustrated with the men who flew the airplanes into the Twin Towers on September 11, 2001. They gave up their bodies but obviously did not believe they would die a psychological or spiritual death. Indeed, many religions speak of an after life on another plane or dimension.

Since it is a belief, it has to be a psychological idea, or a thought, that does not think of its non-existence. Clearly we are attached to the idea that we exist and will continue to exist. This is the function of the creator-god. It rules by fear, but does not want you to cease existing. It knows if you ceased to exist, then it would cease to exist, and that, it will not do. It will create any system of belief to insure that you and it will continue to exist. It can create a heaven or a hell. It can create a story of reincarnation. It can create an idea of an eternal bliss. It can create a belief that you will one day reunite with your ancestors and loved ones. It can create anything, because that is what it does!

In fact, it must convince you that something here in this world, be it as abstract as a belief in a god, is so absolutely true that you dare not give it up. You must hold on to it because it is essential to your identity and survival as an entity. By so doing, you fully identify with the belief so it can continue to exist.

For example, everyone has something they think is so real and true that they dare not give it up for anything or under any circumstance. The Pope dares not give up his belief in Jesus. The Moslem dares not give up his belief in Allah. The scientist dares not give up his belief in the scientific method, and the atheist surely would not give up his belief that God does not exist. Each belief is precious to the individual and gives him or her an identity that sets him or her apart from others. By so doing, these individuals, as well as you and me, obey the commandments of the creator-god. We fight for our survival and fear the loss of our most precious possession – our identity as thinking and believing Beings.

But what is basic to this fear of loss? Where does it come from? How did it evolve? This question will take us to our next commandment.

The Creator God

VII. Commandment

You will believe that all human form has lack and loss as key components of its identity.

In my Psychology and Spirituality class at Morehouse College, I explain to students that almost all known religions have a creation story. Each story began with man in a state of perfection and then experiencing a loss of this perfect state. Of course, we in the Western Hemisphere are most familiar with The Genesis account of Adam and Eve and their departure from the Garden of Eden.

On a more personal level, you and I are familiar with the experience of having been in our mother's womb where we had all our needs met. Although the living quarters may have been tight, we had twenty-four hour room service, perfect body temperature, and constant protection and safety. We were, in a sense, in a state of bliss until the nine-month cycle expired. Then we were thrust into this world kicking, screaming to signify that something had changed. We wanted the world to know something was lacking and something was lost. And, this has not changed since the day of our birth.

We live in a constant state that lack and loss are ever-present companions, always there to remind us that our condition is not complete. Rarely are we in a state where we can relax into the moment and know all is well. Instead, life is spent seeking something more, something better, and something different. As a result, we grow up speculating that the grass is greener on the other side of the fence, and we develop an urgent need to cross that fence from time to time. That is the commandment of the creator-god that is founded on lack and loss. It cannot be complete like Infinity, which is only whole, only complete, and not missing or desirous of anything. Since you and I are products of the creator-god, we feel that we are missing something – never satisfied and always seeking more.

I can recall the day after I earned my Ph.D. Before obtaining my doctorate, I was extremely motivated to accomplish my goal. By God, here was a Black man from Alabama who would rise to the top and earn a doctorate from a predominately white Ivy League School. Watch out world! Here I come! Yet as the creator-god would have it, once I obtained my Ph.D., I became depressed because the world didn't open its arms to me. The earth kept revolving and my world felt the same. My Ph.D. became to me like Linus' blanket was to him in the Peanuts cartoon strips. It was my security blanket, and I became attached to it.

Earning my Ph.D. didn't rid me of my feelings of lack and inadequacy. Since the commandment of the creator-god says lack is always present and we are always seeking. I began to believe that if I became a famous psychologist, my world would be better. Of course, you can guess the outcome. I didn't become famous, but more importantly, I was on a never-ending journey to find satisfaction but never could. This is because the basis of our identity is lack and therefore, we must always maintain our belief in lack in order to claim our identity. The commandment of the creator-god has been obeyed.

Some of you may be asking if this commandment means we will always be lacking in life and never satisfied. The answer is both yes and no. As long as we identify with the creator-god and accept that we are merely human, we will feel lack. We will always be motivated to try something new. For instance, we will always want a bigger house, a faster car, or more money. We have security blankets that give us momentary respite from the never-ending cry of lack and loss. But deep inside, we know that we cannot escape because the ultimate loss is death, and this death, we cannot escape.

As humans, we lack the knowledge that we are whole, complete, and Infinite. This knowledge is the Truth, but the various little gods that rule our minds will not let us recognize this for what it is. We are left feeling a deep and gnawing sense of incompletion. It is this incomplete feeling that is trying to get our attention, calling us home again – like a little baby feeling it is safe and peaceful in its mother's arms. Home is where we belong, where we feel comfort, acceptance, and love. Home is where there are no cares or worries. Home is where we originated – it is from which we came. Home is where heaven is – it is a kingdom that the human mind knows not of because it is beyond our ability to conceive. But it is our home, and all we have to do is be like the prodigal son that Jesus spoke of and go there.

We must know that we have a Father who will welcome us unconditionally no matter what we think we have done. We must be willing to see that we are always connected to our Father. We must be willing to give up the idea that we have been cast out of His home because of our guilt. Once we do so, we will walk into our home and know that we are whole, complete and not lacking in anything. This home is heaven!

I realize this is difficult for some of you to accept. It was difficult for me to accept initially. My puny little mind responded, "Returning home can't happen for me because everything I tried didn't usually turn out well and besides, I don't really deserve all that good stuff." Again, this type of thinking, which I am so familiar with, is a direct result of the false gods and their commandments, particularly the creator-god that has another commandment to ensure that we don't believe that going home is possible. So, let's continue looking at these commandments that obscure our vision of our true identity.

The Creator God

VIII. Commandment

You will believe that all human form must have a cause and each cause must have an effect.

As I mentioned earlier, my father was an educator who had advanced degrees in chemistry. As such, he had a love for the scientific process. As a child I would ask Santa Claus for chemistry sets. After receiving them, I would set up my chemistry labs in the basement of our house. At an early age I grew to love and appreciate science and was fascinated. I took pleasure in questioning my father about the cause of certain effects. Naturally, my father's who thoroughly enjoyed my questions rewarded me.

This process of asking questions has remained with me and interestingly, is the cornerstone of our academic and technological societies. Our society loves cause and effect, and science is here to prove that cause and effect are vital to the functioning of all life. Indeed, religion also worships at this altar stating that God is the ultimate cause. Western religions state that we reap what we sow, and Eastern religions proclaim the Laws of Karma, a similar principle that reinforces the idea of cause and effect. In fact, it seems that all philosophical, theological, and scientific systems are in agreement on the issue of the vital importance of cause and effect. The creator-god's commandment seemingly goes unchallenged. But is this ultimately true? How does the creator-god use this commandment to further its objective of making us believe that it knows what reality is? Let's look further.

In order for cause and effect to occur there must be a time sequence. Cause must come before effect. A causes B and A happens before B. Let me give you a more concrete example; I hit you and you respond. A happens before B in time. But, what if there is no time? What if there is only now? Please try to entertain this possibility? I know it is difficult for the human mind to let go of time, but the Truth is: there is only now. And, now is not in time.

Now just is. Time is something humans experience. We experience events in a sequential manner but the Truth is: there is only now. Stick with me. For example, what time is it now? Don't look at your watch. All you can say that is absolutely true is that it is now and it is now everywhere. It is now on Venus, Mars, in the next galaxy, or millions of galaxies away. It is now and it is always now, but we don't experience our world as such because the creator-god created time. Once time was created, cause and effect were created, not just to have time, but to guarantee that events appeared separate. A causes B and therefore A, although related to B, is also separate from B. Cause and effect are thus events in time.

Now I think I can hear some rumblings that may sound like, "So what?" That is too abstract for me. What does it have to do with my everyday functioning?" Good questions. If you were to consider that there is no cause and no effect, then you must entertain that you have not sinned and are not guilty and therefore do not deserve punishment. This is because in order to sin you must have a cause and an effect. Sin is a judgment called wrong, and then another effect called punishment. But if there is no cause then there is no effect or act that can be judged sinful, and hence, no punishment. I know this is radical for it undercuts all the premises of the creator-god, but please consider all possibilities. Cause and effect are so crucial to the functioning of the creator-god that you and I believe we deserve what we get.

To illustrate, I had a female client who had committed adultery. She came to me experiencing extreme guilt, remorse and depression. As we discussed her affair, she stated that she felt so cheap and low for engaging in such an act. She felt that she could never be forgiven. Although she was able to rationalize to some extent her reasons for the affair, she felt guilty and needed to be punished. And punished she was, mainly by herself and her judgments. She felt her life could never be happy again, and although she was religious and believed in forgiveness, she felt she had to pay a price for her sin. Her price was depression. As we discussed her need to blame herself (the effect), she was able to see that it was her judgment of her behavior that contributed to her depression. Judgment was just a process her mind initiated in childhood to perpetrate her belief that every sin must be punished.

Now, I am not suggesting that people not be held accountable for their actions, especially since this is the way the world operates, but I am suggesting that the creator-god will push the cause and effect commandment to the point where blame is constantly taught and sought, making it difficult for us to be free. We seemingly are caught in the cycle of act and reaction or in Eastern terms, the Karmic cycle. Regardless, the creator-god wants us caught up in cause and effect and therefore, never knowing the freedom that is available for us. We will be unaware of the part of our identity that says there is no time and hence no cause and effect - that we are free from the chains of cause and effect and can soar like eagles high into the sky. We won't know this as long as we remain slaves to the cause and effect commandment.

This commandment appears so sacred and so true. Are there other commandments that we think are true but keep us bound in the prisons of our minds? Well, let's journey on.

The Creator God

IX. Commandment

You will believe that life has a purpose.

For over 25 years I have taught in college settings and have heard many students lament that they didn't know what their purpose was in life. Often they stated their parents wanted them to choose a certain profession that they didn't feel drawn toward. They felt they were floating through life not knowing which way to turn or where they were headed. At several junctures in my life, I experienced similar feelings and therefore, could identify with my students. It does appear that life has a purpose and we are here to find it. We feel it is the fortunate person who truly finds his/her calling in life. So we ask ourselves, "What is the purpose of life" or more specifically, "What is my purpose?"

The two questions appear related, but in actuality they may not be. It may be a trick of the creator-god to keep us stuck in a never-ending struggle of trying to get somewhere that is unattainable. So, let's examine this commandment a little closer and see if we can detect how we may be caught in a cycle that will not allow us freedom.

The debate about the purpose of life has probably been going on since man began to wonder about the origin of life. The most accurate statement we can make about purpose is we don't know. Who can say with certainty that they know what God intends? Who would be arrogant enough to think they knew the "Mind" of Infinity.

Even if we thought such, we would have to admit that in order for God to have a purpose, He would have to have a motive. Purpose is dependent upon motive. As defined by Webster, purpose is the object toward which one strives. In order for God to have an object toward which He strives, He would have to be separate from that object and not possess it. God would have to know of lack and be incomplete and if God is incomplete then He is not All or Infinite. It is as if one took a circle and cut out part of it and said it is a circle. It cannot be a circle because a circle is unbroken. It is complete in itself and if a slice of it is taken away, it is a partial circle – no longer whole or complete.

However, the creator-god tells us that life and God have a purpose, and we think it is true. We spend our lives caught in a web, trying to abide by God's purpose and judging others and ourselves by this purpose. We are caught in the human game, assigning purpose not only to God, but also to everything else in life. We wind up feeling we must have a purpose, and our most basic purpose is to find our purpose. And, when we don't, we usually wind up feeling less than successful or even depressed.

For example, I had a client who was the son of a very successful family. The family had high expectations of him. He was very intelligent and had attended one of the best preparatory schools in his state. However, when he entered a prestigious university he stopped attending classes and eventually flunked out. He started seeing me because he felt he had failed not only school, but also his parents. As we delved into this issue in therapy, he came to see that he had unconsciously created a purpose, which was to totally rebel against his parent's expectations. His life's purpose was to prove to them they could not control him. He was trapped because his purpose was to resist his family. He felt he couldn't just be whom he was.

As we talked more in therapy, he was able to grasp that his mind, either consciously or unconsciously, had made up a purpose that was running his life. I explained that one of the functions of the mind was to create a purpose to motivate us and that this is neither bad nor good; it is just the function of the mind. Since the mind has to create purpose and motivation, he may as well have it create a purpose that would free him. And, so he did.

Eventually he discovered he loved art and began to devote himself to it – this endeavor allowed him to be free. His purpose then was more satisfying and enjoyable. Can I say with any certainty that was the purpose of his life? No! I don't know what the purpose of anyone's life is. I can only make it up. I can create it, hopefully with as little influence from the creator-god as possible.

In fact, I have made up a purpose for my life and that is to discover Truth. I don't know if I will ever do so, but it is something I made up because it gives me some joy and excitement. But, is this my ultimate purpose? Who knows? Is it your purpose? Who knows? It is your life! You play it any way you want to. Just try to remember that the creator-god and other psychological forces seemingly are present with their rules and commandments to define you, as they want.

So, questions may therefore arise such as: "Do I have any freedom? Can I really choose?" Well let's find out as we go to the last commandment of the creator-god.

The Creator God

X. Commandment

You will believe that each human form has free will
and free choice.

This commandment is probably the most sacred one of the ten and it is no accident that I chose it (Did I say chose?) to be last. Gosh, it seems I cannot get away from the idea that I as an individual human personality can choose. It is so basic to the way that I think and function that I cannot believe I cannot be without it. And that's true; humans cannot function without the basic belief that we have the right and power to make certain choices. Didn't I choose to sit down and write this book? Surely, I chose to put on the shirt that I am wearing. No one told me to pick out this red (yes red, and it is a bright red at that!) shirt from my closet and put it on. No one held a gun to my head and made me do it. It was my choice or so it seems. But let's look at this and see if I did have any freedom in my choices or if you have any freedom in yours.

Think about a decision you have made. It can be a selection of a mate, a career or just buying your car. To make this interesting, let's say that it is your wife or husband. You can say you chose to marry him or her freely. But, what made that person appeal to you? Was it their appearance, their intelligence, their way of handling themselves? Regardless of what it was, you were taught what was valuable and what was attractive. Without question, past conditioning influenced that decision, and none of us is fully aware of the extent our past conditioning plays in our lives. We are forever linked to our conditioning and it is this conditioning that tells us what we like or don't like, how to act or not act, who is important or who's not important.

Of course, some may say that they have broken away from their parents, teachers or other people who conditioned them, but how can they be sure to what extent this has happened. Even the language that you and I speak comes from past conditioning. I speak English simply because my parents and other important people around me spoke English. Not only did I learn words and their meanings, I also learned subtleties, values, and the method I use in processing information.

These lessons are always with me and influence the way I interpret my world. My mind is, therefore, always looking out from the past, attempting to interpret the present and anticipate the future. It is the past conditioning that will influence the decision I make in the present. I am never in the present. I always come from the past looking into the present and future.

There is consequently no room left to be in the present, which is the only place a true choice can be made. A free choice is unaffected by any past or future events. It stands alone in the present, free and unencumbered by any conditioning from any other time or event. It is, as the word implies, free choice.

To take this point of free choice or free will a step further, I would have to say that in order to have free will, I would have to have the power to execute this free will. Some action has to occur from my free will. It is a volitional act. It involves the power to decide. The key word here is power. Do I have the power to decide and act? If I had free will, I could do so.

However, if we return to the definition that God is Omnipotent or All-powerful, then where does the power to act come from? If God is the only power, what power is left for you or me? Can you or I have any power separate from God and God still be All-power or Omnipotent? I say no! A resounding no! I know this is a hard pill to swallow, probably the hardest, for us as humans. We base almost everything in our world on our ability to do, to act, to create or to choose. And, this idea of being powerless or impotent is abhorrent to the human mind.

What was Jesus thinking when he said, "Of myself I can do nothing, and It is the Father within that does the work"? Clearly he was pointing to his belief that he, Jesus the man, could not perform any act unless it was a spiritually derived act. All acts for him had to have a spiritual source – the Father within. And, the Father within was the source of power, for all power belongs to and is of that Father or God. No other power can therefore exist. Any power that does appear to exist is just that – an appearance, a mirage, a fake and not a real power.

It is, as some sages say, an illusion created by the mind to perpetrate the belief in a power other than God. And this is just what the creator-god does. It is the trickster that cons us into thinking that there is something other than God that we as humans can have. It tricks us into thinking that we can have a power separate from Omnipotence. We think power allows us to choose something other than Omnipresence – that which is everywhere present and all-powerful. This, of course, is impossible!

The world of the creator-god is an imaginary one, which you and I think we live and struggle in. This, my friend, was the beginning of all mankind's suffering and it continues today with most of us being totally unaware. Quite a marvelous trick. Quite a wonder. Quite a tragedy, unless we are willing to see the creator-god and the other false gods for what they are.

Let's continue our journey to uncover the other false gods of the mind that have us trapped in this thing called I.

Chapter 9

The Ten Commandments of the We-God

The Ten Commandments of The We-God

    I.   You will believe that the group is more powerful than you.

    II.   You will believe that the group provides structure and order for your safety and growth.

    III.   You will only be aware of limited, fear-based love rather than Infinite, true love.

    IV.   You will submit to the ideas and values of authorities that are defined by the group.

    V.   You will let the group define your god and how to worship it.

    VI.   You will be taught the values and rules of the group and accept them as the basis of your identity.

    VII.   You will believe that you belong to a group with a history that shapes your identity.

    VIII.   You will believe that other groups are different and are superior to or inferior to your group.

    IX.   You will feel threatened by other groups and believe you are justified in attacking them.

    X.   You will know freedom only as defined by the rules and expectations of the group.

The We God

I. Commandment

You will believe that the group is more powerful than you.

All of us are born into and function in some group, be it a family, community, tribe, society or nation. We are always a member of some collection of Beings and identify with it. From this, a concept called "we" evolves. "We" refers to a group of individuals that sees and defines itself as a collective body. This collective body or group has a function, which is to exist and to perpetuate its existence. The group has an identity and yields influence and power over those in it.

How did the power of the group evolve? And, why do we give power to the group? The answer can be found at the very beginning of human life. Every human is born to a woman. While residing in the womb of its mother, the fetus is totally identified with the mother and has no existence apart from her. The fetus and the mother are one. The fetus eats what the mother eats. It goes where the mother goes. There is no separation. Once the birth occurs, the infant is separated from its source and the basis for "I and another" is found.

The baby, although at a primitive level, is aware that it is separate from its source, demonstrated by the mere sound of its cry. The cry confirms that he/she is no longer connected continuously to his/her supply source. If the baby had an understanding of arithmetic, he/she could mathematically state that $1+1=2$. Baby being "1", plus another "1", mother, are now two separate entities. The formation of a "we" has begun. There is an "I", although primitive, and there is another that is not "I" or "me." They are no longer one. They are now two.

As the baby develops, the two expands to three with daddy. Then three expands to four and five with other relatives. A family is formed and the family becomes part of a community. Mathematically it can be viewed as $(1+1)N=2N$ with the N representing an unknown number will make up the world of the infant. The infant is now a member of a group. There is a "we" and it begins to wield power over the infant. The infant is totally dependent upon the others for its survival.

This dependency means that the others supply the infant with its nourishment, both physically and psychologically. The infant looks to the others for food for its body and acceptance and assurance for its mind. The others, in particular the mother, father and in some instances guardians or grandparents, become identified as the supply source for the infant's physical and psychological needs. They acquire power over the infant simply because the infant cannot physically or psychologically thrive without them.

I realize that this process is not earth shattering. It is basic human knowledge, but something starts to happen as the baby begins to grow. The others no longer appear to exist only outside of the baby. The baby begins to develop psychological attachments to the others, to the extent that they are brought inside his mind and begin to form a part of his human psyche. In other words, the child has psychologically incorporated a part of mother, father, grandparent or significant others within him and made them a part of his personality.

Traditional psychology has many terms that refer to this process such as internalization or introjection, but my point is: those others are now a part of the child's identity and function as powerful influences over his life. To illustrate, several years ago I was counseling a couple. The wife expressed her dissatisfaction with her husband because he was distant and inattentive to her. As a result, she became disinterested in sex and felt that anytime the husband initiated sexual activity, she was being manipulated and unappreciated.

When I gathered her history, she told me that she was a daddy's girl and felt her father had treated her like a princess. He was very attentive to her and made her feel special, something her husband failed to do. Her father's influence was now playing a powerful role in her marriage, without her knowledge. All she knew was that her husband didn't treat her right. Her first group interactions with her family were still with her psychologically as an adult. In fact, we must appreciate that when we marry, we not only marry that individual, we also marry that individual's family and other groups they identify with.

Each of us is part of a "we" and that "we" has power over us and will control our very likes, dislikes, interests and passions. Because the "we" begins its influence at such an early age, it is the very basis of our personality and controls us in ways that we are not aware of. As life progresses, many others influence us and they become our we-god. The influence of these others is cemented deeply in our psyche, and we rarely are free of their power. It is the role and function of the we-god to insure that we yield to its power. This process begins with this first commandment.

Now let me show you how the we-god controls us and keeps us from our true freedom and the knowledge that we are all one.

The We God

II. Commandment

*You will believe that the group provides structure and order
for your safety and growth.*

In my Psychology and Spirituality class at Morehouse College, I always emphasize that freedom is one of the most precious virtues and all people must be free. Rarely would you disagree with such a noble statement, but you may believe being free does not mean you can do whatever you want to and whenever you want. A basic belief that most of us accept is, "One has to be responsible to the rules of society, for without rules there would be chaos."

This is true only because we identify ourselves as humans and humans appear to be separate entities that interact with each other. Such interactions usually require order and structure and as a result rules are formed. These rules lay the basis for an orderly process, insuring that the group survives and functions productively. All groups have rules. They may be explicit or implicit, formal or informal or a combination thereof.

In my class, I like to use the analogy of what I call the six-point game. In the great American past time, football players compete with each other to score touchdowns. A touchdown is worth six-points. Why six points? It seems one point or even two points is more practical. We can only assume that the founders of the game of football arbitrarily selected six to represent the basic score. It had to be arbitrary, because any number would work. Nevertheless, if we want to play football, we must know and accept the fact that a touchdown is worth six points, and this is a rule of the game that we must follow if we want an orderly game.

The same is true in our lives; for the most part, our lives are a play of the six-point game. In order to thrive in the game, we must know the rules and realize that it was made up by others to perpetuate the game. And, in the game, there are winners and losers, or so it appears. The difficulty comes when we begin to believe that the game is real and we start to think of ourselves as winners or losers.

There was a time in my life that I believed winning was all important, and I had to be, "king of the mountain." For me this meant playing the game called success. And, I played it well for a time. I achieved goals, became successful, and was viewed by others as a winner. I told my sons that when they accepted a job they should learn the rules of the game and observe how people played it at work. Good advice, right? Yes, for the six-point game, but I hadn't realized that the six-point game had begun to consume my life and was in fact defining me.

I really thought that my very Being depended upon my success in playing the game. Particularly the 'game' called psychology. My identity was now being defined by the game and my success playing it. The we-god was alive and thriving. However at night, I was sleeping less. I was experiencing more anxiety, and I noticed that I wasn't really happy.

The six-point game makes winners and losers, but not truly happy people. The structure and order of society is to produce successful and productive citizens and not people who are truly aware and truly loving. And, that I was not.

The six-point game, which is a function of the we-god, is designed for its survival. If we comply and submit to its rules and structure, we will never know who we are or what true love is. True love is only of God – that which is Infinite and beyond the structure and rules of the we-god. We may know and participate in the six-point game of the we-god, but we must be aware that it is just a game and it does not define us. Who and what we are transcends all games, all structures, all rules. For we are Infinite – far beyond anything that the we-god can structure, although it still attempts to do so. So, let's continue to see how!

The We God

III. Commandment

You will only know of limited, fear-based love rather than Infinite, true love.

I remember a lecture from graduate school about Abraham Maslow's Hierarchy of Need Theory. The theory identifies five levels of human needs. The first and most basic need we have is survival. We have a built in survival mechanism and, like all organisms in their natural state, we will attempt to survive. Survival, of course, implies that there is a threat to us. Non-survival or death is always present. We see death as a threat and fear it.

The second need that Maslow identifies is the need for safety. If there is a threat, then there is a need for not only survival, but also safety. The need for safety implies that we can be un-safe or threatened. Fear again makes its presence known. Anthropologists and sociologists often state that animals form groups not only to survive, but also to insure their safety. Fear must be dealt with and a group may be better able to deal with fear than one alone. The positive motive, therefore, for forming a group is for survival and safety, but the negative aspect is it insures fear will continue to exist.

We cannot have a concern for survival or safety without being aware of non-survival or un-safety. Societies and groups must know that they can be threatened, eliminated or destroyed. Fear is therefore, the condition that all humans must exist within, either on an unconscious or on a conscious level. Maslow unknowingly identified that the basic need for survival insures that the fear of non-survival exists. Likewise, the need for safety must also have the need for un-safety. The positive has to include its opposite, the negative, simply because they are connected. To have good, we also must have bad. The law of opposites has to exist in the world of the creator-god and in the world of the we-god.

As a result, the group or society always contends with fear. Even when it speaks of love, which should be beyond fear, the group or society manages to connect fear with it. I recall as a child being taught by my grandmother and pastor that I should fear God. This fear was so pervasive that I was afraid that God would catch me doing something wrong and punish me. I was so terrified of God that I dared not place any items on top of the Bible for fear of God's retribution. My family and society had taught me that God, who was to be loved, was also to be feared.

Indeed, the fear of God became a virtue. Many times, as a child, I would hear my elders describe a respected person as a good God-fearing man. In my mind, good Christians feared God. Love and fear were connected. No wonder we have so much trouble loving. We have heard too many contradictory messages about love, especially relating to God and fear.

Often as a therapist, I have seen clients profoundly influenced by this confusion of love and fear. I recall a woman who was raised in a family where her father and God were powerful figures who engendered fear in her. She recalled being beaten by her father for not remembering her Sunday school lessons correctly. She stated that God was someone that she was afraid of displeasing. Not surprisingly, it was vital that she did the right thing for fear of punishment. As a result she was highly anxious, particularly about failing. Failure to her was going to hell and when she did fail, she psychologically sent herself to hell. She was extremely unhappy, and made those around her unhappy to the extent that her husband divorced her, and her children were constantly in trouble at school or with the law.

It took awhile for her to see that the abuse from her father and the teachings she had about God were keeping her imprisoned in a fear-based love. As therapy progressed, she came to see that fear is just a condition of the mind. Her experiences of fear molded and shaped her perception of self. She had not considered the option that she could love and be loved unconditionally.

It is not the objective of society or the we-god to make us aware that perfect love has no conditions and knows no fear. Perfect Love or Infinite Being doesn't know of the existence of fear to cast it out. Infinite Love is Infinite. It has no boundaries. It knows no opposite. It cannot be aware of fear. It is the we-god along with the creator-god that must say differently, which they attempt to do so with their commandments. If we are to be free and love unconditionally, we must free ourselves from these commandments, or we will be forever bound by them. So, let's continue with this journey.

The We God

IV. Commandment

You will submit to the ideas and values of authorities that are defined by the group.

The idea of authority seems so real that it defies questioning. Everywhere we turn there is some authority dictating to us, commanding us, ordering us or judging us. We go to work and are met by our boss who wants us to do something. We drive our car down the highway and immediately slow down when we see the blue lights of a police car. We call our parents and even though we are adults, we are still treated as if we are children. Authority, authority, authority everywhere!

As we exit our mother's womb, we are issued into the world of submission to authority. After our mother, we are introduced to our father who **really** must demonstrate his authority – because he is a man. Men are taught by society that to be a man they must wield authority and power over others, particularly those they see as weaker and smaller.

Our world expands from our parents to other relatives and then to school where we spend a major portion of each day. We submit to the rules of teachers who attempt to teach us the curriculum of selected subjects that was chosen by some unknown authorities. After school extra curricular activities lead us to other authorities such as athletic coaches and band directors who attempt to further educate us in selected activities.

Not to be surpassed, yet clearly an authority is our relationship with religious leaders. Religious leaders are certainly authority figures, and also carry the ultimate power of being a spokesperson for the prime authority – God. Our lives are over-run with authority figures. Is it no wonder that so many of us are told we have an authority complex? Single black mothers, who are looking for a black male therapist for their adolescent sons, frequently call me. They feel that their sons need a black male therapist, stating that their child, "just won't mind them and beyond that they think they are God." They are described as "just having too much mouth and not respecting authority."

African-American boys are not the only ones who have an authority issue. We all have authority issues. We have all had experiences, good and bad, with authorities. We may rebel against them as the adolescent sons referred to me do, or we may readily submit to them and not "show any trouble." But, however we have experienced authority, we really do not know true authority. Our experiences with authority have been in the world of the we-god, where the group has defined the authority and we have been conditioned to accept it as such.

They are authorities because someone said they were and we accepted it. But who gave them that authority? How do you know what the authority proclaims is true? Who said it is true? Can they demonstrate it is true? These questions need to be considered when you are confronted with a predicament in your life and feel trapped.

For example, I once saw a woman in therapy that had been married for over ten years. She had two children and felt her husband no longer loved her because he was having several affairs. She wanted to leave the marriage but believed that a divorce would permanently scar her children. So, she stayed in the dismal situation. Her belief had become an authority not to be questioned. She unquestionably submitted to it and had not asked the pertinent question: "Who told you it was true and how did they know?"

After inquiring, she saw that she had acquired the belief from her mother and community. There was an unspoken expectation that 'good people do not get divorced'. For her, the we-god was very much alive and demanded strict adherence to its commandments.

This inquiry process threatens the we-god. It does not want its commandments to be questioned, for it may be unmasked like the wizard in the Wizard of Oz. But, the Truth is, the we-god is not the authority that has power over us and by questioning our beliefs and ideas we can know this. It is the desire to know the Truth that will impel us in our lives – for

Truth is the only authority. Truth is true – anything else is a lie and no lie can live forever.

A lie can only exist if we give it authority and power. It continues to exist if it is not questioned or examined. Truth will stand under examination, questioning, and investigation. It can withstand any process because Truth is eternal and unchangeable. Two plus two equals four - always! It is eternal and unalterable. It cannot be changed because it is true.

So question any concept, belief, idea or commandment of an authority. This is a particularly noble act if your intention is to find Truth and not just an act of defiance. By questioning every sacred idea, every belief, every authoritarian statement you have been given by your family, church, or community, you can begin to see through the conditioning. These groups or institutions may have been well intended, but often the leaders seen as authorities have never questioned the source or validity or their beliefs.

When you question and inquire, Truth will reveal itself. It has to, for only God is Truth and God cannot withhold Himself from you – not an Omnipresent God. He is never beyond your reach. **That** is what Truth is and **that** is the ultimate authority. It is only conditioned beliefs from a creator-god and we-god that seemingly block out this Truth. Let's continue on this journey and find out how this blockage occurs.

The We God

V. Commandment

You will let the group define your god
and how to worship it.

At this stage of our journey, I would like to ask you a question. Can you think of a society that does not have a religion or a spiritual system with at least one deity? I realize that there are some religions that are not as theistic as the Western religions, but can you think of a society that does not have a spiritual or supernatural belief system about a Being with super natural powers? The answer is no. All societies have some system that addresses the super natural or what is often termed the spiritual. They must because all societies are composed of humans with limited knowledge, and humans must have a system to explain the unknown and the unknowable. That's how the need for god was born.

What about the need? How is this god defined? The definition may vary from culture to culture, but clearly this god possesses attributes and qualities that are superior to humans. Humans, therefore, do not see themselves as possessing these attributes and conclude that god is external to them and more powerful. By definition, this appears to be what a god is or at least what we think a god is. This seems reasonable to us because we are aware that we are limited. We see our bodies as limited because they appear to deteriorate and eventually die. That is our experience as humans, but God doesn't die. God may not have a body or form, and appears to be immortal – beyond the grasp of death and time.

However, it must be pointed out that these are all concepts. They are ideas that we have about the unknown and it is the society or group that defines this unknown for us. Once god becomes a concept, we can think of it, worship it, even visualize it, and have, of course, a relationship with it. There is a god and me relationship – two separate ones interacting together. And, our minds are conditioned by our societies, families, and institutions to worship this god.

In the Western religions, god is the ultimate authority. Society has formal religious institutions to guarantee that we worship god in a prescribed and proper manner. To question the authority of god or its institutions is called heresy, and you will be punished if you disobey.

There are numerous examples of this in Western history. The one that comes to mind is Galileo and his devotion to the scientific method and its discoveries. By stating that the sun is the center of the solar system, which was contrary to the church's teachings, Galileo was placed under house arrest and never able to experience freedom again. The we-god does not tolerate deviance and defiance.

While reading about Galileo's struggles, I recall thinking that the church was so unfair in its judgment of him. I took a position and judged the church wrong. Now, I realize I was participating in the same process that I condemned. I thought I was right and the church was wrong. Believing that I was right and judging another wrong is a process that the human mind seems to have to engage in.

Most humans psychologically worship the same "god" and unknowingly make it an authority and that authority or "god" is called, "I'm Right." I knew I was right about the church. It was clearly unfair in my eyes. But, the church thought it was right also. Most of us need to be right and often take on, should I say, religious conviction about it. Our politics, our religion, our ideas are right, at least so it seems to us. But right has to have its opposite – wrong. And once right and wrong are established, conflict must follow.

Yet, one that is Infinite does not have an opposite – and once I engage in being right I have left the domain of the Infinite (as if that is possible) and entered the world of the human mind with its creator-god and we-god. This is so easy to do, so very easy, because I just love being right. Even as I write these commandments, I believe that I am right! It is just the way it is, or so it appears to this little mind of mine.

However, there is a world that is true. It is the world that Jesus referred to in his statement: "My kingdom is not of this world." How do we get to this kingdom? Is it even possible to obtain when the we-god seemingly controls the way we see, think and are with god? Again we must proceed on this journey. We must become more aware of the obstacles that prevent us from seeing the Truth.

The We God

VI. Commandment

You will be taught the values and rules of the group and accept them as the basis of your identity.

It is appropriate at this juncture that we encounter the one commandment that could allow us complete freedom and the ability to know who we really are. No kidding! The basis of our identities is rooted in this commandment. It addresses all that we value, and all the values that we think we are grounded in. Our society teaches us standards by which we judge others and ourselves. They are viewed as valuable and meaningful. We invest in them. We think they are good and right. And, out of these standards comes our ability to determine what is good; what is right; what is bad; what is wrong. And we judge. And we judge. And we judge. The human existence is built on judging. And judging is built on standards that we think have value.

If we look deeper, we will see that there is no inherent value in any thing, any person or place. Value is not found within anything. It is only an idea we ascribe to something. It does not reside within any object, person or place. It only resides within our mind, placed there by some institution, group or other individual. Once it becomes a part of our mind, it seems valuable to us because it gives us standards we can use to evaluate others and ourselves. These standards are, therefore, the foundation of judging, which is the primary activity of the human mind.

Just think about it, you and I have opinions about almost everything. In particular, we have opinions about what we hold dear. We will literally fight to the death for what we hold dear. It seems right to us and gives us a purpose for our lives. Without values, what meaning or purpose would our lives have?

I recall an incident when I was in middle school. Like most middle school youth, I admired the high school students and thought some of them were so cool! In particular, I remember a person who was the star of the football and basketball teams. He had the reputation of "being bad." His teachers saw him as arrogant for he often defied them. But, as a young impressible adolescent, I thought he was "cool."

On one particular night, this young man, let's call him Leroy, was in the unsavory part of town. He had a few too many drinks, and got into an argument with someone, knocking a bag of popcorn from his' hand. As Leroy turned away to walk to the other side of the street, the other young man pulled out a gun and fatally shot Leroy in the head. When questioned why he had shot Leroy, the young man said he felt disrespected and he could not tolerate anyone disrespecting him.

Sounds silly doesn't it? On one level it is silly and reprehensible that one person would kill another over a bag of popcorn. But, the point is that the young man had an idea, a self- concept, a belief that he held dear and had invested in. In other words, his belief was so valuable that he was willing to kill. Never did he stop to examine his belief. Never did he question any aspect of it, whether it was important or not. He was operating on automatic. His beliefs, which he thought were valuable and meaningful, were running his life.

Of course, most of us would not kill another individual, especially over a bag of popcorn. Nevertheless, my point is that most of us operate on automatic. We have beliefs that we think are valuable because they give us a purpose and a meaning in life. These beliefs tie us down to them. They become so important that they literally define us. Rarely do we question them. In a sense they take on a life of their own. We see the world through that which we think is important. And, we will defend what we think is important.

A threat is only a threat because it challenges what we consider valuable. For example, if I was to take something from your garbage can, you perhaps would not feel particularly threatened, because your garbage probably isn't considered important. However, if I took something from your wallet, you would probably feel threatened and defend yourself and your wallet. The contents of your wallet are valuable. The garbage is not. Values determine our actions and perspective on life.

Where do these values come from? How did you know money is important or that your education is important? The answer, of course, is someone taught you. A two-month old baby does not value a hundred dollar bill. His parents have to teach him that it is valuable. Perhaps your parents use to repeatedly say, "Money doesn't grow on trees." In this message the lesson is clear. Money is valuable. It is part of our conditioning. The we-god dictates to us what is valuable and what is important. We learn our lessons well, sometimes too well, like the young man who killed Leroy, and operate on automatic, never questioning our value system.

What if we did know that values are only important because they perpetuate certain standards and behaviors in society? What if we could see that no value is inherently true? Could we envision that? Is it possible for us to be free from the conditioning of the values of our society? Would we want to be free from our values anyway? What would our lives be like if we didn't have values? Would there be chaos and anarchy or mass confusion? These are all good questions and deserve to be answered if we are to explore the inner sanctums of our minds and challenge the various false gods that command our world.

The answer is simple: as humans, we will have values. We will have standards. We will have rules. As humans, we cannot escape from values because the human mind must judge, and society will teach us what to judge. Society will perpetuate itself by projecting what it considers valuable at almost any cost. Pick up today's newspaper, and you'll se what is important to society. Wars are fought because one group says something is important as opposed to another group that says something else is important. The economy runs on what people invest in, and people invest in what they deem important. Even the newspaper headlines are because the newspaper editors decided certain topics are more important than other topics and should be given the headlines status.

Values or needs are important and, therefore, inescapable in this human world. Yet, what is more significant is the way we relate to what is considered important and the purpose it is playing in our lives. We must examine these values, determine how they originated, what part they play in our lives and why we are attrached to them.

For example, the Klu Klux Klan thinks it is important that Black people and other minority groups are treated in inferior ways. Because these beliefs are important to them, they respond and treat Black Americans in a particular way. Their values serve the purpose of making them feel important and superior. They relate to their values as if they were sacred and unquestionably true. Thank God most of us don't share the same values as the Klan, but what we all share with the Klan members is that mechanism that makes us cling to our values. This mechanism, given to us by society, is attachment to and non-questioning of our values. Indeed, we are often ostracized or threatened with some punishment if we question the most sacred values of the society or we-god.

We have forgotten that values are not inherently valuable or even true. They are valuable only because someone said they were. That someone may have been an important person we deemed to be significant such as our parent, teacher or preacher. We accepted what they said, and by doing so, we adopted their values, and we now contend that this idea, principle or belief is valuable.

"We" are now saying so. "We" are now giving it power. But in reality, it has the power because we have not examined it, and we are chained to it because it has become valuable. Freedom comes only when we question the value, see its origin, see why we are attached to it and understand the role it is playing in our lives. We can continue to hold values and let them operate in our lives, but we do not have to be slaves to them. If we are to be free we must see what holds us down and keeps us bound. We are held down by the values of our society.

What's wrong with that, some of you may ask? Isn't the alternative chaos and total hell? Not necessarily, it is not that we are not to have values; we are to see how we are attached to them. And, we can only know this if we are willing to question these values.

To hold any value or belief as sacred and unquestionable makes it a sacred cow and this we cannot afford. Sacred cows can run amuck in our lives. They must be controlled. We gain control by questioning and using them rather than letting them use us. We can have freedom with values, especially, when we realize their importance is not inherently factual. They only have worth because we say so. We have the opportunity to break free from our slavish attachments to our conditions, beliefs and principles. Consequently, we will be more open, more receptive to what is real, true, and not bound by past conditioning. When this happens, we are available for the present moment, which is true freedom – the freedom to be who we really are.

The We God

VII. Commandment

You will believe that you belong to a group with a history that shapes your identity.

If you think you are human, and who doesn't, then you belong to a group. It is just that simple. Just being human puts you in a group called human. Once you belong to a group, you have a history that is associated with that group. Humans have a history, called the history of mankind.

The human group however, is just one group that you and I are members of. Think about it. Just off the top of your head, you can probably name at least three groups that you are a member of simply because you exist. You had no choice. Once you were born you were automatically a member of some groups. For example, I am a male, an American, and I am Black. All three groups were simply given to me by my birth, and all three groups have histories that contribute to my identity.

The group's history plays a critical role in creating identity. History is not only a record of past events; it is a story that has psychological significance for the group as a whole and for each member. The group gives each member a psychological home. It says we belong. We are not isolated. We are connected with others. We share something in common. We share an identity, and we share a common history. The history links us together, creating a bond between us.

Not only is there a bond between the present members of the group, but also a linkage to members called ancestors or pioneers. They are viewed as having paved the way for present members and are usually given homage and respect. I can remember my father speaking proudly of Frederick Douglas and E. B. Dubois. As Black men who paid a price for Black people's current status, my father would say, we owed them a lot, and we stand on their shoulders. Quite a tribute! There is a need to acknowledge those who have contributed to our present day status. However as the mind would have it, a subtle but powerful trick is involved in this process.

The mind loves the past and indeed is embedded in it. Honoring our ancestors may be appropriate, but it can also keep us stuck in the past. The mind does this by using a group's history to make its members believe they have been treated unfairly. Each group has a belief that another group, at some time, has treated it unfairly, and it is the group's ancestors who have sacrificed to ensure the survival of the group. This process guarantees that one group will remain separate from another group, will feel "less than" that group and will need to compensate for the unfair treatment its members have received.

This principle has clearly influenced my life as a Black man growing up in Alabama. I need not enumerate the ways that Black people have been unfairly treated in America. They are too numerous and obvious to state. Black people have been and still are being treated unfairly. That is a historical fact! Yet, what's important is whether that historical fact empowers or imprisons me. I can recall coming of age in the 1960's and feeling proud that after being denied any sense of self-respect and decency in the 1950's, White America was coming to see the emotional pain and suffering of Black people. We had been systematically dismissed in history books or simply lied about. Thus, the 60's and 70's were an oasis for me as I learned of the many contributions of my ancestors.

However, as I stand some thirty years later looking over my psychological development as a Black man, I see that it was important that I learn the whole and complete Truth about my past. Now I realize that it is even more important that I learn how to relate to my past. For if one is not careful about the past, it can be like hugging an octopus. It will grab you more than you will grab it. History is a story of the past, and the mind under the direction of the we-god, must keep you in the past.

In my particular case, I see that believing that I am a Black man who has been unfairly treated is a story that will imprison me with strong emotions that keep me in the past, feeling separate from other groups. I have now come to the realization that it was necessary for me to grow from being inferiorly passive and afraid of White people to acknowledging my anger and rage for their past injustices. That was psychologically healthy and allowed me to embrace more of the Truth.

What can be psychologically unhealthy is my need to keep my history before me as the basis of my identity. If I think that the unfair treatment of Black people is crucial to my identity, and I underline the word crucial, then I cannot get out of the past. The past of Black people then becomes my octopus. It has grabbed me. If, on the other hand, I can see the past as simply a story that must be told Truthfully and is a part of my human identity but does not **define** me, then I can release myself. Then I can see that I may have a past, but I am not my past.

When we can see that no group, be it national, racial, religious or even family, is the basis of our identity, but only contribute to our experience of our world, then we are free to be who we really are – children of God who have Spirit as the basis of our identity. And Spirit does not belong to any group. Spirit can only be in the now and is not shackled by past or even a future. It just is! That is our identity!

Does this mean that I do not consider myself a Black man and am unaware of the horrors of Jim Crow and racism? Of course not! It is necessary that I am aware of it all, and know all that has happened to my people and me in the "game of life." I must know the pain my ancestors suffered. I must know the ugly faces of racists, be they K.K.K. members or men in suits in corporate America. I also must know that this is part of the human game and I will play it and play it hard, always keeping in the forefront my awareness that I am Spirit. Only Spirit is true and that is what will make us free. That is what will liberate us. And, that is what will liberate all groups and unite them into One. Yet, more barriers remain to keep us from knowing this. So, let's continue to explore these barriers created by the we-god.

The We God

VIII. Commandment

You will believe other groups are different and are superior to or inferior to your group.

As I sit here writing, I glance over at the newspaper and see the sports section. In big bold letters the headlines state, *The Final Four is Upon Us,* meaning only one college basketball team will reign supreme. I think back to just a few months ago and recall the day in January, which has become a sacred holiday in America, Superbowl Sunday. One team and only one team alone emerged as victor – the "best". The other team suffered the agony of defeat and has to wait until next year to prove they are worthy of the title of being the best, of being number one.

However, is the battle to prove that one team is better than another just reserved for sports? Often it is said that sports are just a metaphor for a country's values. In many ways that is true. I can recall playing basketball in high school. My team had a cross-town rival. I feared this team because they had guys from the "hood". Guys from the "hood" were known to be tough and to do anything to win. We felt we were not as tough as they were but surely would not let them know it. We certainly had to try to win and occasionally we did. Now, isn't this the name of the game? Isn't winning what it is all about, especially in this competitive, capitalistic society of the West? Doesn't God have to win over the devil? And, isn't our team or group better than some other group or team?

Judging from appearances, this may be true. It does seem that life is structured around one team or group deciding it is better than another. Throughout history, wars were fought to prove that one side was superior to another. This was especially important if God was believed to be on the winning group's side. God must bless that side because it was just and right. The world is built around the belief that a superior group is better than an inferior group. However, we have a problem. No group wants to feel it is inferior. Being inferior hurts and no group, in its right mind, likes pain.

When I was a child, I recall being told by my light skinned relatives that I was too dark skinned and had a wide nose, which was unattractive. The pain of being labeled inferior by my own people because I didn't look European was so intense that I vowed I would show those who hurt me that I wasn't inferior. I would show them that I was smart by making good grades. This attempt to show them was a compensation or, in psychological terms, a reaction formation. It was an attempt to deny the pain of being labeled inferior by trying to become equal or superior.

I have also seen this dynamic in several of my African-American patients. I remember a young, successful, dark skinned African-American who was referred to me because he was depressed. Bill, as we shall call him, had all the symbols of success. He had a beautiful family and wife (that he liked to boast was light skinned, with flowing hair), a six-figure income, an expensive car and a large house. His life was filled with special activities that only men of his status could afford. He was driven to always be number one. On weekends he entered bicycle races and became known as the best in his age category. Winning was important to him. Indeed, he often said that losers always finished last.

In therapy, I attempted to get underneath his need to achieve, and finally, in one session he revealed his pain. He felt his mother had rejected him because he was too "African looking", and he could not tolerate this pain. He often expressed anger toward Black people, especially those who, in his opinion, were not motivated to succeed. Sadly, at this point he discontinued therapy, and I heard a few years later that he had died prematurely of a heart attack. His attempt to avoid his pain had probably contributed to him paying the ultimate price.

Although we may feel pity and sadness for Bill, at a deeper level we can see that he represents many facets of what the we-god or society teaches us. Clearly, there is a belief that others must be made inferior to us. Bill believed he was inferior because of his color. Obviously, Bill believed that his mother instigated his inferiority complex. Realizing how painful it was to feel inferior, Bill developed a need to demonstrate his superiority over others, including White people but more importantly over, as he termed, "low life Negroes." He had to have an inferior group; even if it was the group he was a member of.

In fact, this story demonstrates that the need for superiority is directly related to feelings of inferiority. Although they look different, they are related and indeed are one and the same. The inferior group has been singled out as different, 'less than' and is judged to lack something. The superior group also feels it is different but is convinced it is 'better than' because it can judge the inferior group as 'less than'. The superior group is dependent upon the supposedly inferior group for its status. Bill's feelings of superiority and need to achieve were rooted in his feelings of inferiority.

What if the Truth is: there is **no** difference between inferiority and superiority? What if this is another judgment of the mind to ensure that the groups remain separate and unequal? This question is not merely a question. If properly considered, it can lead to discussing the Truth. In Truth all groups are the same or one. No one group is better or less than another. Truth cannot make this distinction. Only the human mind, with its little creator-god and we-god, would engage in such senseless activity.

The creator-god and we-god are masters at making us feel separate. It convinces us that our families, ethnic group, race, political party, and religion are the best, and we are unaware that we are judging others to be less. When this occurs conflict arises and justifications are made, which guarantees the survival of the creator-god, we-god and i-god. The story goes on and on, unless we come to Truth and realize who we **really** are. This cannot be accomplished until we discover more about the workings of these various false gods.

The We God

IX. Commandment

You will feel threatened by other groups and believe you are justified in attacking them.

Growing up during the Cold War era of the 1950's, I experienced the threat of the build up of missiles to defend America against the Soviet Union. As a college student in the 1960's, I participated in the civil rights movement and experienced White racists threatening Black people's demand for equal rights. In history classes, I read about the Jewish struggle against Nazi tyranny and understood their need to establish a Jewish state. Today, I see Palestinians hurling bricks at the Israeli army who are viewed as Jewish invaders and occupiers of their homeland.

Seemingly, conflicts never end. One group feels threatened, justly or unjustly, by another group and must defend against or attack that group. Such is the course of history; it is the commandment of the we-god. We should attack any group that threatens us. It seems so reasonable. So, rational and so indubitably true.

Yet, is it rational? Is it indubitably true? Why does the human mind have to continually play scenarios that involve an 'us' versus a 'them'? If we examine this question we will discover several common factors inherent in all conflicts. First, I identify with a group that is different from other groups, as stated in the 8th commandment. Second, the group that I don't identify with, I see as a threat, simply because it can take away something that my group deems important and valuable. Third, once the opposing group attempts to deny or keep from my group that valuable component, I would experience loss.

Once loss is experienced, I feel deprived and must blame someone. Once blame is established, guilt is present. With guilt as my motivating force, I can attack the other group because they are guilty. They are guilty simply because I have judged them as wrong. Clearly, they are wrong because I have lost or been denied something valuable or important. Now that guilt is present, my group and I are justified in attacking the opposing group.

Attack is therefore justified in my mind, and if the authorities in my group sanction the attack, then I am fully supported and justified. And, that is the way of the world and the story of mankind. The we-god reigns supreme.

What if there is another way? What if there is no need to attack a threatening group? Does this seem reasonable? To truly answer this question, I must ask you to go beyond what is reasonable, expected or seemingly natural. The answer to this question lies beyond what is predictable and fathomable by the human mind. The answer to this question can only be found outside of the customary way of looking at yourself, your group or the world.

As a Black man who is aware of racial bigotry, both subtle and overt, and who has experienced its effects, I know this can be difficult to do. I can recall feeling an intense rage toward White people on April 4, 1968, when Dr. King was assassinated. I felt that all was lost for Black Americans. Black people needed to retaliate for the senseless death of 'our leader'. Burn cities down! Hell yes! Let those people know that we are tired of their bigotry and racial injustices. Attack, no matter how futile, was justified to me.

Although I have matured somewhat since 1968, there was still a smoldering resentment toward White people for what they did to my people and me. Any time a Black person was able to retaliate, even if it was in symbolic ways, such as Mohammad Ali beating the man at his game, I rejoiced, openly or silently. It just seemed warranted to me. We could not be passive any longer. We could not let White people dominate and treat us less than human. The keyword is – human.

As long as I continued to identify as human, be it Black or whatever group, I would feel threatened because there is always that underlying belief that my group and I have been treated unfairly. My group would teach me that I had been denied or deprived, and I would accept that these acts by the opposing group were unjust. That is the basis of the sad human story.

To escape from this story, I realized that I must get outside the story and the storyteller. I have to discern that my True Identity is not human but Spiritual. I have to see that who I **really** am is love. And, if I am love, then I am one with all others. That would mean no group is separate from me.

As I began to consider this option, white racists came to mind – the very ones who had killed Dr. King, and the ones who had kept me from attending their schools. As I contemplated, I saw that they also felt deprived. I realized that something inside of them was missing and they were afraid. They were afraid of me, a Black man. You see: attack only occurs when one is afraid. Once I saw this, I realized that we all thought we were deprived of something. And, that something was Love. Hence, love cannot fear. Love is total safety. It casts out fear, and as one great writer said, *Where Love is, fear cannot exist*. Where Love is, unity is. Where Love is, there is freedom.

That is what I had to realize. That is what I had to come to see. Yet, it is difficult. The pull of my group identity will always set me up to feel threatened and have the need to defend and attack. Does this mean that I deny my heritage and identification with Blackness? Of course not. Just as Jesus didn't dissociate himself from being a Jew, we should not deny our heritage. Indeed, what Christians celebrate as the last supper was Jesus celebrating a Seder feast as part of the Jewish Passover holiday.

The key is, to question how strong the hold is that the group or we-god has on me. Does it grab me and totally define what is true and real, or does it simply serve as an instrument to guide me through my daily activities? Herein lie my dilemma and my work. I must consciously, and I stress consciously, commit to and seek what is **true**. I must totally commit to this as an act of declaration and put the we-god on notice that what is most important to me is Truth.

By taking such a stand, I will see Truth emerge, for Truth must reveal itself. It is the only force that is Absolute. Anything other than Truth is a lie. A lie only has power if I give it power by believing in it. Truth does **not** require belief. It just is. Therefore, I must question the beliefs of my group or we-god and see if they stand up to Truth. If they don't, why would I hold on to them? I must let them go, even if it is a painful and soul wrenching process. Truth is certainly worth it! This has to be my commitment, and if you are desirous of freedom and love, it must also be your commitment.

We must be willing to look within and without and question all that we have been taught or have identified with to discover what is true. If we don't, then history surely will continue to repeat itself, and there will always be an 'us' versus a 'them'. Now, to hasten the day when we will overcome this barrier, we must continue on this journey and come to the last of the barriers erected by the we-god.

The We God

X. Commandment

*You will know freedom only as defined by the rules and
expectations of the group.*

The word freedom – how sweet and precious it is. It is so
sweet and alluring that almost everyone cries out for it. Wars
are fought for it. It is such a precious commodity that if we did
not have it, some of us would surely die. However, most of us
are the walking dead, because we do not understand or have a
full grasp of the Truth about freedom. If fully understood,
many of us would change our minds about freedom and trade it
in for more familiar and comfortable companions. For sure,
some of us would exchange safety and security for freedom,
because **freedom demands holding onto nothing**. To be free,
one has to allow all to be as it is – no attachment to any
judgment or standard. Freedom is unbounded, untouched and
unattached. It is simply that – **free**.

This type of freedom can be frightening to the we-god.
Society must have rules, standards and expectations in order to
function. And, society will function regardless of our desire to
be free. Society or the we-god gives us standards because it
must have structure. With these standards, limits are set,

thereby placing a restriction on freedom. Freedom is no longer unbounded. Freedom is now a concept used for the purpose of society or we-god.

Society tells us that to be successful, we must accept its standards and definition of success, and submit to its rules, which may often entail forsaking what we truly desire. I recall seeing a middle aged Black woman in therapy. She complained of being depressed and unhappy with her career. From a very early age, she was encouraged by her father to become a teacher, nurse or secretary. These professions, he explained, would guarantee her a steady income. This was not an uncommon expectation for young Black females in the 1950's and 60's.

Black society expected them to earn an income but only in selected fields. Her desire, however, was to be an engineer, a career reserved primarily for males. She didn't feel free to do or be what she wanted. She acquiesced to the demands of society and became a teacher, but underneath she resented the restrictions that were placed on her. She met the standards and expectations of her society but at the price of not being true to herself. Consequently, she became a depressed and angry individual, feeling imprisoned.

In therapy, I asked her several times if she would consider changing careers to pursue what she really wanted, but this seemed inconceivable to her. She often responded by asking,

"What would my family or neighbors think? What would they say?"

Herein lay the power of the we-god. "What would they say" – the infamous and ever seemingly powerful 'they'. The 'they' seems to have the ability to judge what is right or wrong for us. The 'they' sets the standards and defines what we should do, how we should act and what we should think. The ever present 'they' – the we-god. The 'they' that constantly asks us to submit to its will, its standards, its rules, its judgment, and its commandments.

What if the "I" within us cries out for its expression? Can we allow ourselves to fully and freely express who we are, or do we willingly submit to the supposed authority of a 'they' – the seeming power of the we-god?

If we are to love ourselves, we must **really** honor ourselves. To honor ourselves is to realize that we are truthfully free – free to honor what is real, what is authentic. To be truly free, we must make the basis of our identity - our true self that is given to us by God – the self that is not defined by an external force or group. It is the self that is pure and undefined because it is of God.

It may be likened to that essence that Jesus spoke of when he said, "Except ye be as a little child, ye cannot enter the kingdom of heaven." The little child is natural. The little child is open. The little child is eager to discover the world in an uninhibited fashion. This little child is so in touch with its source that it just lives in the moment, not judging but totally accepting. Unless we allow ourselves to be as the little child – that which is natural – we will imprison ourselves in the rules and expectations placed upon us by others.

If we don't become as little children, we throw away our freedom and ability to be truly in touch with what is Real. This is too high a price to pay. The we-god must be dealt with and seen for the imposter it is. It is designed for its survival even at the price of killing what is most precious to us – our natural and authentic self, which yearns to be free.

We therefore must ask ourselves daily, which god are we serving. Do we serve a god that demands and commands that we sacrifice what is authentic within us, or do we serve a God that allows us full freedom to be our true selves? This ultimately is one of the most basic questions we can ask. If we are really open to the answer, the authentic and loving God will give us our freedom to be our **true selves**. And, what greater and more loving gift is there?

Chapter 10

The Ten Commandments of the I-God

The Ten Commandments of The i-god

I. You will be unaware of the connection of all forms to Oneness.

II. You will believe that you are your body.

III. You will believe that you are unworthy with a guilty and shameful past.

IV. You will fear an ultimate authority and attempt to please, avoid or love this authority.

V. You will believe you lack love and structure your life around this lack.

VI. You will create romantic relationships to express love, hate and fear.

VII. You will see life as a struggle and create a story to justify that struggle.

VIII. You will see the solution to your problems as external to yourself.

IX. You will engage in meaningless activity, believing it has value and purpose.

X. You will never know the Truth.

The I God

I. Commandment

You will be unaware of the connection of all forms to Oneness.

If I asked the average man or woman on the street what's true to them. They would probably say, their god is true and they exist. If I asked them what's real to them. They would probably answer, this world is real, objects are real and all that they can see is real. With further questioning, they would also say that not only are these tangible objects real, but also they are different from one another. For the average Joe or Jane on the street, this seems unquestionably true and real. This is not to be questioned. This is never to be assumed otherwise.

However, is this the case? Is reality composed of separate and distinct objects that have little or no connection with each other? Everything does seem to be different. The average Joe or Jane would say, "My eyes do not lie to me. Seeing is believing and that's the Truth." An elephant and mosquito are obviously different and bare little, if any, resemblance to each other. This is obvious to everyone. The i-god is apparently correct. Things are different and if there are connections they are few and tenuous.

The world is built on differences. In fact, we learn through comparison and contrast – a process that emphasizes differences. I am different from you, and you are different from me. I share some things in common with you, but we are essentially different, or so I think.

As I examine closely, in thinking or believing that I am different, I can see a very powerful process at work. For example, if I think I am different from others, I must also say that I am **unlike** them, and therefore, cannot do the things that they do. This process of separating and disassociating myself from others may serve to keep alive certain beliefs and concepts about myself. It may help me identify attributes within myself, particularly if these attributes are judged as negative.

Recently, I witnessed this process very vividly. I've been a customer of this particular bank for twenty years, and am very familiar with the tellers and manager. However, as I was standing in line this particular day, a thought crossed my mind. It said, "Why don't you rob the bank?" Of course, I immediately rejected the idea and did not rob the bank (thank God). But, the importance of this story is that I realized that I could be a bank-robber. There was very little that separated me that day from the bank-robber that is sitting in jail. I am like him in some ways. After all, we shared similar thoughts, with the exception that I did not act out mine.

Yet, I want to deny that I could be such. I don't want to see myself as being such a negative person who would rob from others. And even worse, could I be so connected to these negative thoughts that I could be like Hitler, the K.K.K. Grand Dragon, or even the devil? Perish the thought. No way, would I dare to believe I could be as such. It would destroy all that I think of myself, and I dare not let others imagine that I could think or be such.

However, if I am to have it all, I must be willing to be it all, including the negative and the positive. I must be willing to see that I am connected to all that is negative, and that I am capable of doing the most dastardly acts. In so doing, I can bring forth compassion knowing that but for the grace of God, there go I. I can put myself in others' shoes and realize that I live in a glass house and cannot afford to throw stones.

Compassion arises that acts on my reactive tendency to judge others as 'less than'. It breaks down the barriers between others and me and allows me to join with them in spirit, realizing that we are one and are only different at the level of human thinking or judging.

However, this process should not be limited to joining with those we consider negative or less than. If I can be like a Hitler, the logical question that should arise is whether I also can be like positive beings. In other words, can I be like Gandhi, Martin Luther King, Nelson Mandela or even Jesus? The point arises that if I am to have it all, I must be it ALL. I must see that not only do I possess the most negative attributes; I also possess the most positive ones. All cannot be limited. It must include everything to be all; otherwise it is not all.

I, therefore, must allow myself to think that I can be a Martin, a Gandhi, a Nelson Mandela or even a Jesus. If they were capable of doing such, why shouldn't I? What is important to stress here is that these individuals clearly stated and knew that their power to be such positive individuals was solely based on their willingness to submit to a higher spiritual power.

Their personal i- god would not and could not take them to greatness. Greatness was not what they sought. Instead they sought to surrender their personal desires and ideals to their spiritual source. They knew that their identity and power were spiritually based and not psychologically defined. They had to go outside of their usual way of thinking and enter a realm where they did not matter; only the Will of God mattered. This is our task. This is our purpose. This is our goal. Once we see that we are connected to it all, we will see that we are all. We are one. Is there anything else to see or be?

The I God

II. Commandment

You will believe that you are your body.

Probably the single most important idea to my mind is the belief that I am somebody – I am a physical being, who was conceived from the union of two bodies and will interact with other bodies throughout my life. This "I" that I think I am, is totally identified with this body. In fact, I have a special day each year that I celebrate the introduction of my body into this world. My birthday is simply the recognition and verification that my body is basic to my identity. I believe my body is the I that I am.

When asked to identify myself, I usually show a picture of the upper part of my body as proof of my identity. When my body demands certain things, I respond to its demands. When my body is hungry, I will feed it. When it is tired, I will rest it. When it is in pain, I will try to reduce the pain. And of course, when it wants pleasure, I will try to get another body to join with it hoping to satisfy it. The body not only appears to be me, it rules me. It is the focus of my life, and I must listen to it, or I will suffer and die.

I can recall seeing a patient whose life was totally centered around her body. Each day she would rise in pain and program her activities around doctors' visits and taking her medications. Most of her conversation revolved around her physical complaints, and she never tired of letting others know of her pain. Her physician referred her to me because there was little medical basis for her condition. When I would raise the possibility that her pain could possibly not be medical, she immediately rejected the idea and felt I was not being sympathetic.

This type of individual is not foreign to most of us. Often we know people who are so immersed in the aches and pains of their bodies that we avoid them. We don't appreciate it when people remind us of the suffering and pain the body can experience. It makes us aware of our own limitations and pain. However, we love it when we can discuss improving the body, how to overcome our weight problems, or how to make our bodies more beautiful, younger or sexier.

We dare not think of the termination of our bodies – our death. We push away the thought that our bodies are programmed for self-destruction, are temporal, vulnerable, and can fail us at any moment. The thought of death causes us to live with a constant undercurrent of fear. Death becomes the ultimate fear, for we believe we will no longer exist when our body dies.

Yet, this belief that seems so real can be examined, as any belief can and should. Is the body the basis of who I am? Is this skin bag, that I identify with and allow to determine almost everything that I experience, really my true identity? Until we ask these questions, we are doomed to experience a life of limitation, lack, pain and loss, punctuated by a few moments of brief pleasure. If we had any degree of wisdom, we would be willing to examine this most cherished belief of ours.

This brings to mind a young lady that was referred to me for therapy. She was experiencing depression related to drug abuse. She began to use drugs when she was a dancer in one of the local nude clubs. Drugs served as a way of anesthetizing her experiences in the club. She stated she felt like she was being used as an object and was not fully appreciated by others. She was an intelligent and perceptive person and was a student at one of the local colleges.

As she related her experience as a nude dancer, she uttered a very profound statement, "No one has ever seen me." This woman's nightly job was to strip naked before others, allowing them to view every inch of her body, but she was clear that while they were looking at her body, they were not seeing her. Who she was went beyond her body. Her **true self** was invisible to the human eye. Her **true self** transcended the material, the carnal, and the visible. Her **true self** was not limited by the usual definitions. She had created the possibility that her identity was not encased and limited to her body and therefore, she could allow for the emergence of other possibilities.

The pull to totally identify with our bodies is so strong and pervasive that we create religions that do not challenge the centrality of the body or the manner in which the mind uses it to perpetuate the belief in separation and suffering. In fact, suffering often plays a vital role in theology. For example, the most sacred holiday in Christianity is Holy Week when Christians believe that Jesus suffered a painful physical death and arose later in a form that is unfamiliar to most of us.

As a young Christian man, I can recall hearing the story of the Garden of Gethsemane. I was confused by the agony that Jesus supposedly experienced. I certainly believed Jesus had performed miracles, such as walking on water, turning water into wine, and returning Lazarus from the dead. Why then, would He experience such agony and ambivalence at His impeding death?

Why would He allow Himself to identify with His body when He was aware that His identity was Spiritual? Hadn't He stated that He and His Father were One? Was death and bodily pain really something for a spiritual master to fear? The answer became clear, as I understood the nature of the universal mind and its false gods. They have a need to project their view of the world.

Death of the body cannot be fearful to Spiritual Beings because their reality is purely non-physical. Death is only fearful to those who are not immersed in the reality of the invisible. The human mind is afraid of its death because it fears. And, its greatest fear is the death of its body, which is inevitable. Jesus, however, knew His identity was not physically or psychologically bound.

If He struggled at all, it was because He was still clinging to His personal identity, the i-god. Conversely, this was impossible, because He was a spiritual Master that did not obey the commandments of the i-god. He was fully established in his identity as a Spiritual Being and was incapable of allowing His body and mind to control His true reality. The struggle we read about was not His struggle, but the projected belief of those around Him who did not understand spiritual identity. They were only able to see and understand a reality they knew. They were caught in their human identities, like most of us.

We, as humans, have little understanding of this process and must, under the directions of our limited finite minds or i-god, make even the spiritual look like the mental and physical. This is why we are taught that Jesus suffered and agonized over and during his death. Jesus therefore, becomes like us rather than we becoming like Him.

To be Christ like, we must see that our true identity lies in the invisible rather than a bodily form. The mind or the i-god must be challenged. It must be examined and discarded so reality and Truth can be recognized. Jesus knew this Truth. He knew His true identity was the invisible presence that can only Love and be Love. He knew Love could not be contained in any physical form. And, He wanted us to know, dear reader, that this is also our true identity. For we are Love, the only power and presence there is, and not a body.

The I God

III. Commandment

You will believe that you are unworthy with a guilty and shameful past.

I imagine some of you found the concluding statements to the previous Commandment somewhat upsetting. To state that 'You and I are the Christ' may sound blasphemous. No doubt, at some point in history, I would have been put to death for making such a statement. Just imagine, you or me being the Christ. No way! We believe Christ is Jesus, and he died for our sins 2,000 years ago. However, Christ is only a title. It was not Jesus' last name. It indicated that he was the enlightened one, the Savior. He was in a perfect relationship with his Father, and They were One.

Why would the title Christ be reserved for one man? Could it be possible that we are all capable of joining with the Infinite? Is that possible? What prevents us from becoming this Light, this all-encompassing power of Love? To answer such a question, we must begin where all barriers and doubts occur – in the mind, which includes the personal mind or i-god, the social mind or we-god, and the universal thinking mind (the originator of separation) or creator-god.

Basic to all these minds that are within us is the core concept of sin or guilt. It is the belief in sin or guilt that forms the basic structure of the human condition. This belief is buttressed by many of the world's religions, which teach that man is born in sin. Man has done something wrong and as a result he is guilty and unworthy of being loved. This belief lies deep within the unconscious of all humans and sets the stage for all human interactions.

Although we may not be fully aware of this core belief, we experience it on a personal level through the feelings of inadequacy or shame that play out in our relationships. As children, we desired the love and approval of our parents and engaged in behaviors to get their love and approval. However, our parents were not just parents. They were also engaged in other roles such as spouses, providers or community leaders. They attempted to love us as best they could, but their love was not consistent or unconditional.

Therefore, we did not get the love that fully supported us and let us know that we were accepted no matter what we did. As a result, we doubted not only our parents but also ourselves. A decision was made unconsciously that something was wrong because we did not get the love we wanted, and we, therefore, were the cause of it. This decision parallels with the story in Genesis when Adam and Eve realized that they had done something wrong and deserved to be punished.

Like Adam and Eve, our unconscious mind decided we did something wrong and, therefore, we were wrong. We unconsciously pronounced ourselves guilty and not deserving of ultimate love. Being not deserving of love, we find ourselves on a continuous quest to find love but never fully attaining unconditional love.

We feel guilty for acts we believed we committed, as well as things we should have done. It is equivalent to the religious teachings of sins of omission and commission. I am guilty for what I did and did not do. If you were to really be honest with yourself, you would have to confess that you have self-doubts and are afraid that others may find out that you are not as good as they think you are. In other words, in the vernacular of the streets, "We fake it, till we make it", and we hope others won't find out. Does this sound familiar?

A patient of mine, who is a young African-American female and successful attorney, came to me after her husband of eight years decided to leave her. Prior to this, her best friend had also broken off their relationship. In our sessions, the woman tearfully stated that she felt empty inside and was frightened because she had to face life as a divorced mother with two small children. As she related her history, she shared that her father had left her when she was a young girl, and she always wondered if she had done something wrong to make him leave.

She suppressed this guilt, and it resurfaced in her marriage and turned into depression. She felt inadequate as a mother and wife, despite her significant professional accomplishments. She realized that her achievements were defenses to shield her from deep feelings of inadequacy and guilt, her core beliefs about herself. Fortunately, she was able to work through these beliefs and feelings. Soon she began to grasp that love is not dependent upon others. She began to understand that love is what she is.

Yet, the human mind argues strongly against this knowing. It will bring up incidents and stories from our lives and make us relive the pain of the past. At other times, it will bury them, making us forget. Yet we have a deep, gnawing sense of discontent within that we don't understand. To help us deal with this discomfort, the human mind will offer us refuge by blaming others or keeping us emotionally distant in relationships. These are only quick fixes. The pain of guilt, shame and inadequacy remains, and we are stuck.

The only way out, as many sages have taught, is to forgive. Forgiveness is the only cure for guilt and shame. But, to be effective, forgiveness must be understood. The forgiveness that I am speaking of does not entail just simply releasing another from what you consider to be their wrongdoing. This does not eliminate guilt, because your perception of their wrongdoing is what established the guilt in the first place.

True forgiveness recognizes there is no guilt and never was! People just do what they do. Behavior is neutral. It is our judgment that makes the behavior right or wrong. It is the commandments of the we-god, the creator-god and the i-god that make us believe we are guilty. Infinity cannot judge, because It would have to have another and there is only one Infinity – not two. And, that Infinite One is the I that I am. None other.

Yet, what about those others who hurt us, who did not love us, who used us, or abused us? What about them? The answer, dear reader, is "Forgive them for they know not what they do," or more accurately, they do not know who they are. They do not know that they are loved unconditionally. If they did, they would not hurt us, abuse us or leave us.

Most importantly we must forgive ourselves. We must see that we are Infinite love and cannot be hurt, and in Truth have never been hurt. We have been misidentified. We thought we were human when in Truth we are Spirit. We are Love. Therefore, True forgiveness begins at home. It must begin with us knowing that we were misidentified, and we thought we were a psychosocial Being with a name attached to a body. As we do this we begin letting go of the guilt we see in others and ourselves. Hence, our primary task is to let go of guilt.

I realize this seems difficult and goes against the core beliefs of our human minds. All the little gods will scream in horror and fight vehemently against us thinking or behaving this way. They would cease to exist! But, so be it. Christ or Infinite Love cannot die or be hurt and that is who and what we are.

Does this sound blasphemous? Does it sound as if you or I are going against God? Should we be afraid that God is going to strike us down or smite us for such a statement? If such is your belief, let's see where this fear comes from.

The I God

IV. Commandment

You will fear an ultimate authority and attempt to please,
avoid or love this authority.

Like many adolescents, I struggled with the decision of a career. At times, I wanted to be a professional basketball player. Other times, I wanted to be a scientist like my father, but I decided in my junior year of high school to be a minister. In fact, I gave a sermon in my church and felt pleased when I was congratulated and told I had "the calling". It was also around this time that I left high school early and entered Morehouse College, a school known for producing great Black preachers and leaders such as Martin Luther King.

It seemed clear, at that time, that I would be a minister. Leaving a small town in Alabama and entering an environment that exposed me to diverse backgrounds was eye opening and challenged my precious religious and philosophical beliefs. Also, at this time my father died, and I realized I was free, or so I thought, of living up to his expectations.

After my father's death, I decided I no longer wanted to be a minister. In fact, I began to question my concept of God. God was a rather distant figure who could be judgmental and whose favor I was not sure I could obtain. God was very much like my father, although I vaguely saw it at that time. As I began to study psychological theories, I realized this insight was not only true for me but was also the basis of Freudian and other psychological theories of religion and God.

When I speak of god in this manner, I am not referring to the Infinite, Unknowable One. I am speaking of the concept of god we **think** we know. Ultimately, a human cannot know God. God is Infinite, and therefore, not knowable to the finite, concept-bound human mind.

The question that logically arises is: "Where did our concept of god come from?" In Western thought, the concept that god must contain a personal element is based on the personality. Our concept of god is directly related to our personalities, personal experiences and personal beliefs, therefore, creating a personal god. Our concept of god must include authority, and god is viewed as the ultimate authority.

In western society, authority figures are usually males and most of our earliest personal experiences with authority are with parents, in particular our fathers. God the father can actually mean god the biological father that we know, or god the sociological father that we are taught to believe in. Either way, god is the result of our experiences with authority and they will determine the nature or personality of this god and the way we relate to him.

My father was essentially a good man but was also distant, feared, and for me, difficult to please. God was likewise an authority figure who was distant, feared, and someone I was always attempting to please. It is no accident that my two primary authority figures were similar in nature. Indeed, for many of us, god is simply an extension of our relationships to our authority figures.

This psychological basis for god would account for the various images that exist within the same religion, church or even family. Everyone brings their personal experiences to their religion and interprets their religious dogma through them, particularly those involving authority. This is how a Unitarian, who is Christian, can have a god that is very different from a fundamental Baptist, who is also Christian. Same Bible, same Jesus, but different expressions of god the authority.

Usually common to these different experiences is a desire to please and avoid disapproval of god the authority. In fact, many religions will use fear as a motivation for shaping behavior. We are taught that god is to be feared, or he will strike us down. Therefore, we structure our lives to please god. This means we sacrifice to avoid his disapproval or to acquire his blessings.

Sacrifice, or giving up something important, is usually a key component. We cannot do what we want. We must be willing to give up in order to get god's blessing. However, is this absolutely necessary? Is sacrifice really required, or is it a trick that the human mind or i-god uses to keep us stuck in the hell of our minds.

I recall seeing a woman in her mid-forties in therapy. She was a good and faithful member of her church and a loyal wife and mother, who always gave of herself first and rarely thought of her needs. When she entered therapy she was depressed, but could not understand why. She had a good home, loving husband, children, and worked hard "doing the Lord's work." Life was about sacrificing herself, and she thought she would be rewarded for such behavior.

Her personal history revealed that she was the oldest of six and was expected to care for her younger siblings. Her father was a stern and strict disciplinarian whom she feared. She was never sure if she did things right. Her mother was a submissive, passive woman who felt controlled and dominated by her husband. The script was well prepared for my client. It was no surprise that her husband was also a strict individual whom she attempted to please.

She was of a fundamental Christian denomination and spent most of her time either trying to please her husband or her god, never knowing if she would succeed. Rarely, would she allow time to nurture and care for herself. Others came first. Her needs were secondary. A perfect foundation for depression.

In therapy, I attempted to help her see that her needs were important, and she was entitled to have freedom, and asserting herself to her husband and god would be psychologically and spiritually healthy. With some reflection she was able to connect her father, her husband, and her god and realize she had made a prison for herself in her mind. She saw that if God is a loving god, He is all loving – no conditions. Just all love. He was like the Father that Jesus related to in the story of the prodigal son who just wanted to be with his children and love them unconditionally. The children did not have to earn His love. They did not have to sacrifice. They did not have to fast or even tithe. They were loved simply because they were His children.

When my client saw this, and I do mean **saw**, when this penetrated into the emotional and intuitive parts of her, she began to smile and stated she felt free – free to be who she wanted to be – free to be her own self. She knew then that she had to honor the ancient saying, "To thine own self be true." For when you are true to your own self, your true self, you will be true to God. You will begin to serve God and others freely and naturally, through the authority or power of unconditional love.

Sounds good doesn't it? But we don't believe it yet. We seem to always feel as if we are missing or lacking it. Now, let's look at this condition called lack.

The I God

V. Commandment

*You will believe you lack love and structure your
life around this lack.*

Somewhere in our lives we have run into that person who
looks like he or she has it all. They look and act so perfect, so
cool, so together. Everything they touch turns to gold. They
can do no wrong or even if they do wrong, it turns into a
victory. I know you know this type of person. We all do. And
the funny thing about it is, although we may envy them, we
find ourselves strongly attracted to them. They seem to have
something we don't have, and we wish we could at least
possess a fraction of their seeming perfection. If only we could
be a fraction as smart, as good looking, as poised, and debonair
as they are. If only.

The longing to be like them clearly indicates that we think
we do not have something that they have. We believe that we
are lacking, not complete, not as good as Mr. or Ms. Perfect. It
seems as if we entered life feeling incomplete, always wishing
we had more of something that we perceive we are missing.

If we only knew the Truth about the nature of the human
mind and the i-god, we would see that the very structure of

everyone's mind is built on lack. Inherent within everyone, yes including Mr. and Ms. Perfect, is the belief that screams loudly that there is something missing. We all feel incomplete and spend our lives attempting to fill this feeling of lack and incompletion. Indeed, this is the basis of all motivation. Goals are simply an acknowledgement that we do not have something and must do something to get it.

Lack is, therefore, the basis for seemingly all goal-oriented activities. Even our bodies tell us that lack is essential to living. Every few hours our body tells us that it is lacking food or rest and will demand that we fulfill this lack. We find food and feed ourselves or lie down and rest. Motivation and lack are intrinsically connected. That's just life, or so it seems.

I imagine some of you may be asking, "What's wrong with that? That is just life – so what!" Granted there is nothing wrong with it, but when we are unaware of the role that lack plays in our lives, we have difficulties and get struck. To illustrate, I saw a man in therapy. He came to me because his wife demanded he seek counseling or she would leave him.

Her complaint was that he spent so much time working, that he had little or no time for her or his family. He reluctantly entered therapy because he didn't understand his wife's complaints. He was a hard worker and prided himself on his accomplishments. Being poor as a child, he was extremely proud that he held a high position in his company. He had made a decision early in life that he would never be poor again, and he kept his promise. He was not poor. He had a six-figure income, a half million-dollar house, belonged to the right clubs and right church. He had made it because he had worked very hard.

As therapy progressed, he shared a pivotal incident from adolescence when he asked "a pretty 'light skinned' girl" for a date. She laughed, and told him he was not her kind because he was from "the wrong side of the tracks and too dark skinned." He acknowledged his hurt, but said he turned lemons into lemonade by resolving from that day forward to be better than she and her kind. He devoted himself to his studies and became hard working and achieved his goal. Indeed, he asked, "What's wrong with reaching the top of the mountain?" "Nothing and everything," I replied.

What's important here is to remember that he felt hurt by the young lady. Her message to him was that he was missing something. He was lacking. His recognition of this lack became a motivation for success and even though it worked, he still was incomplete. The motivation to prove that he was "just as good as" or "even better than" had taken over his life to the extent that he could not fully be with his family. He could not just "be". He had to always "do".

Proving to others that he was "just as good as" became his mountain to climb. And, underneath this doing lay the feeling of inadequacy and lack. The "who" that he thought he was had become identified with his proving success. Little did he know, he also identified with another part of himself he wanted to forget – not being good enough. No matter how successful he was, or how much money he earned, or which clubs he was a member of, he could never be complete or satisfied because his mind was still identified with the pain of lack that had not been healed. Going to the outer to cure the inner will never work. The inner pain must be acknowledged and healed before completion or satisfaction can occur.

Let me give you another example. I had a patient who had begun drinking too much and his work performance was falling off. He was in his mid-forties, good looking and quite charming. He was "a lady's man" and was proud of the fact that he had slept with more women than he could count. He had been married, but could not remain faithful to his wife. His life was centered on "bedding down as many women as he could." And apparently, he was very successful. Yet, he was entering therapy because he was dissatisfied and perplexed with his life.

He was successful professionally, but could not understand why he was not satisfied. His history revealed he was the only male of five siblings. He was raised by his mother and grandmother and, therefore, was surrounded by females. He proudly stated he learned about women by watching his sisters and mother, but he also felt dominated by all the women in his life. He really longed to have a father to help him deal with all the female influence in his life. So, conquering women sexually became a way to escape feminine domination and exerting the power he lacked.

Committed relationships were terrifying because then a woman would control him, and he could not allow that. His sense of manhood and masculinity rested on sexual conquests of females. Yet, this never brought him satisfaction. Eventually he began to use alcohol to satisfy himself, but of course this eventually proved futile. He needed to face the real problem. He had to realize that he had spent his life trying to avoid or fulfill a lack.

The problem with both men from the above examples is that they were not aware of three crucial points. First, the human mind, with its i-god, will always tell us that we are missing something. Second, the human mind will tell us to go outside ourselves and get something to fill the hole or complete what is missing. Third and most importantly, the human mind will never tell us that what we think will fill our feelings of lack **cannot** and will **never** satisfy us.

The human mind won't tell us the Truth about lack, because it **is** lack. It does not and cannot know the Truth. Truth terrifies the human mind. Only the Infinite One is Truth. Only God, Omnipresence is complete, whole, not lacking anything. It is the All. It is the One. It is the Source. It is the Love that we feel we are missing.

The irony is that it is Omnipresent, so how can we lack it? We only **think** we do because we listen to the i-god or the human thought machine and believe it is true and it is us. We must therefore go inside and examine our thoughts, our beliefs, our feelings, and see if they promote lack or love.

When we begin this process we are on the way to freedom from lack and suffering. But, this is not an easy task. It can be frightening to challenge our cherished beliefs about our little psychological gods and ourselves. They can easily distract us. The i-god combines with the we-god to create one of the cleverest distractions known to man, romantic relationships – the sacred cow of the i-god and we-god. Let's examine this distraction in the next commandment.

The I God

VI. Commandment

*You will create romantic relationships to express love,
hate and fear.*

Ah love!   Ain't it great?   Ain't it grand? Ain't it
wonderful? Ain't it awful? Ain't it painful? Aint it hell!!! Does
this sound familiar? Ring any bells for you? When we first
meet that special one, we feel wonderful. We feel great. We
feel as if love is meant for us and our world has changed. Then
something happens. Those magnificent, amazing, grand
feelings are altered. That fantastic, marvelous person, whom
we met and fell in love with, seemingly begins to change.
There are no longer bells ringing and star-filled eyes. The
relationship begins to experience pain. It begins to hurt and
feel awful at times. Indeed, it even becomes hell if we allow
ourselves to admit the Truth.

So, what happened? How and why did that one, who was
once the joy of our heart, become our heartache? What did we
do wrong? Why did that person change? Where did our love
go? These are often the questions that arise as we trudge that
trail of romance. And even though we can't unearth definitive
answers to our questions, we keep trying, hoping things will

change for the better, or we meet another person who we believe will bring us the love we so desire.

Once again, the human mind with its i-god has tricked us. We think that romantic love will make our lives better. But, romantic love **cannot** and **never** will make us better! It is not designed for that. Its purpose is for us to have complaints against another. Sounds shocking, doesn't it? It bears repeating because this shakes the very foundational of our belief about romantic love. The psychological purpose of romantic love is to have complaints and, consequently, it cannot deliver on its promise to give us love. I'll let that sink in slowly.

Allow me to explain, as I'm sure some of you may be reeling from my assertion. I realize this may sound cynical or pessimistic, but the nature of the human mind must be exposed so we can begin to experience the love that we desire and try so hard to attain. Even the statistics about marriage tell us we aren't too successful with this thing called love. Over fifty percent of all first marriages end in divorce, and seventy-two percent of all second marriages wind up the same way. This does not reflect the number of marriages that are unhappy but have not wound up in the legal system. It seems the statistics say that although we keep trying to find true love, we are not succeeding.

Why is that so? To understand we must go to the origin of our experience with love. Every child, when they are born, wants the love of their parents. It matters not if mommy or daddy isn't there. Each child wants that love. The demands of the we-god and creator-god states, "the ideal situation for each child is to have contact and love from their parents." Most of us do, but it often doesn't come the way we want it. It is not unconditional.

Our parents, no matter how loving they may be, cannot meet all our demands. They hurt us, because they are involved in their own lives. We, therefore, feel lack of love and hurt. We try to defend ourselves by repressing the pain in our unconscious. As we mature and grow into adolescence and later adulthood, we meet an individual who has also repressed their pain, which may compliment our pain.

Initially, this person makes us feel good and we think we are in love. We want to spend time with them, get close to them and share our lives with them. So we do. We begin to share, or so we think. There comes a point, however, where the sharing begins to become uncomfortable. We think we cannot reveal certain parts of ourselves, for they will disapprove or, worse yet, reject and leave us.

This anticipated pain of separation could be excruciating, for it unconsciously reminds us of our separation from a once serene state of being in our mother's womb, or our belief of separation from God. This pain is so intense in our unconscious and is buried so deeply that we remain completely unaware of it. This, along with the other psychological wounds we received from parents, siblings and significant others during childhood, is lying there waiting to come out. In an intimate relationship, these feelings will raise their ugly heads. They have to. They must, and sometimes in the most surprising way.

Recently I received a call from the court system asking me if I would see in therapy a 50 year-old female who was arrested for assault and battery. I agreed and was somewhat shocked when I met her. She was a very tiny lady who was devotedly religious. She carried her Bible with her at all times and was easily offended if anyone uttered a profane word in her presence. Yet, she was in therapy for assaulting her husband!

When I gathered her history, I discovered that she was the only child of a mother whom she described as being very passive. Her father was an alcoholic and womanizer who physically abused her mother. She sided with her mother during the parental fights and begged her mother to leave her father. Eventually, her mother obtained a divorce and later remarried a man who didn't drink, but was physically abusive.

My client made an important decision then and vowed never to marry a man who drank or was unfaithful. In fact, she stated one of the reasons she joined her fundamental church was to increase the probability of meeting a man who met her qualifications. She was successful or so it appeared.

She met a man who was a devout Christian and was, as she described him, "a good God-fearing man." They married and she was initially content, thinking that her life was happy and safe. One day she came home early from work and found her husband in bed with another woman. She said, "I snapped and lost it, let the devil take control and began to physically attack my husband." She stated that she felt extremely guilty and ashamed and was at a loss to explain her behavior other than that the devil had taken control of her.

After much discussion, she was able to see that she had experienced significant pain from seeing her mother hurt and the pain had never healed. As a result, it had remained in her unconscious, and when she caught her husband in the act of adultery, the pain resurfaced. The anger and rage she felt toward her husband was also the anger and rage she felt for her father, stepfather and even mother. They had all hurt her and she carried those unresolved feelings of her earlier life into her present situation.

I explained to her that the human mind, with its i-god, is embedded in the past and interprets all present events in terms of the past. The present therefore must resemble the past because the past is all the mind knows. The mind reproduces itself and its basic beliefs so that it can continue to exist. As a result she, as well as most of us, constantly relives the pain and joy of the past.

In order to release ourselves from these intense feelings of anger, fear or loss, we must begin to realize we have had the same feelings in the past and, more than likely, in our first love relationship. When this is acknowledged, we can see that the person we feel anger or hatred toward is offering us an opportunity to look back at the origin of these feelings and release ourselves from their powerful hold.

That origin usually begins with our parents. When we feel deprived of love by the most important people in our lives, we make them wrong and guilty for hurting us. Then we use criticism and blame as defenses to keep from experiencing our hurt. We blame them, consciously and unconsciously. We sometimes blame ourselves. And, as life progresses, whenever we experience these feelings, we project blame onto our nearest loved ones, usually our partner, spouse or significant other.

To illustrate further, a couple sought treatment from me after the wife stated she could not tolerate her husband stalking her at work and embarrassing her in front of her coworkers. She had begun to experience loneliness after being a devoted wife for 23 years, while her husband had several affairs. She began to associate with a coworker for companionship, but never had sexual relations with him. Her husband found out about this friendship and became enraged. He confronted this man at work, publicly embarrassing his wife. She felt it was grossly unfair. The husband admitted the unfairness of the situation, but felt he had no control over his jealousy.

I inquired about his history; he stated he was one of four children raised by a single parent. Even though his mother was devoted to her children, he never felt any warmth or "real nurturing from her." He felt the men his mother brought home received more of her attention than he did. As we talked, I was able to point out to him that he felt deprived of his mother's love and resented the affection she showed other males. He agreed saying, his mother was wrong and she should not have done that.

His feelings of lack or deprivation formed the core for the dynamics of the relationship with his wife. He felt inadequate, not good enough for her love or the love of any other woman. This pain was so great that he repressed it, while unconsciously judging his mother and other women inadequate. He couldn't allow them to see his inadequacies, so he had to control them, dominate them or even punish them.

They were guilty, and guilt always demands punishment. His multiple affairs were opportunities to demonstrate that he was superior to women, and his need to control and dominate his wife was a way to punish his mother for his feelings of hurt and inadequacy. The past had become the present and future. They were all the same to his unconscious. They just looked different on the surface.

I have shared these stories about my clients to illustrate a principle that operates in all of us. That principle is: all romantic relationships are about lack, or joining with another to get what we don't have. We are not fully aware that we believe we are lacking, nor are we fully aware that we believe something is wrong with us at some level. However, we know we are inadequate and hope no one finds out.

Therefore, when we find that special someone, we try not to let them see our inadequacies or they will reject us. We do this by not fully joining with them. We allow them into our lives only to a certain extent. When that level is crossed, we protect ourselves by making them guilty. We attack, blame or criticize them to make sure they don't get any closer. They usually respond with a counter-attack and the conflict has begun. We are now joined by attack, guilt and blame.

By attacking the one "we love", the i-god is successful in achieving its objective. This objective is that men and women will be forever attracted to each other, not by love, but by guilt – a marriage made in the i-god heaven. Sounds awful and depressing, doesn't it? It is if we allow ourselves to remain in the clutches of the human mind or i-god.

To escape from this emotional prison we must only learn one principle. The other person isn't guilty and neither are we. Both parties in a relationship are unconsciously bound by their past hurts. They protect themselves by projecting those hurts and negative feelings onto their partner.

Our relationships, however, can also provide us an opportunity to heal, to complete the unfinished business of our pasts. Our partners act as agents who dig up buried experiences from our pasts and bring them into our awareness. Once uncovered, we can look at them and release ourselves from their control. We can see that the hurts we experienced as innocent children are nothing to be ashamed of; we just wanted to be loved. Our parents had the same experience with their parents, and their parents with their parents, and so on. It can all be traced back to the beginning of all relationships, which takes us back to the creator-god.

So, who is to blame? The answer should be obvious – no one. Not one single person. We are all emotionally deprived children looking for love, not understanding the game that the creator-god, we-god and i-god made. Once we see this we can release ourselves from feeling deprived and inadequate and become healed and whole.

Nonetheless, we usually resist. It can be more comfortable for us to struggle with our partners. We literally hold onto our pain and suffering. But, why do we do this? Why do we choose the drama of fighting, pain and suffering? Because we feel we must hold onto our beliefs of inadequacy and being unfairly treated. We identify ourselves through these beliefs. They define who we think we are and our world. By thinking we are our beliefs, we stay stuck in a false identity. We believe our lives would end without our beliefs.

The Truth is we are not our beliefs. They are only the I that we think we are, the false "I", the psychological "I" and not the "I that I Am" – The Whole, Infinite Complete I that is The All of All, The Beginning and The End. It is our true identity! It is the I that is Love and loved. Isn't that what love is – the knowledge and experience of wholeness, completion, and oneness? Isn't that what we wanted initially from our parents, to know that we were **not** lacking, guilty or to blame? Love has completed itself within us and our relationships, when we know that we are free to be who we really are – loving and joyous children of the true all loving God, sharing and giving to one another.

What a wonderful idea! What a wonderful goal! Is it possible? Of course it is, but we must uncover what else these false gods have commanded to keep us from our true love.

The I God

VII. Commandment

You will see life as a struggle and create a story to justify that struggle.

Movies, soap operas, television dramas – shows that are all stories. Boy, do we love them. They are often so fascinating that we become addicted to them. Soap operas can dominate people's lives to the extent that they forget the stories are fictional. Many of us rush home in the evening because we cannot miss our favorite television drama.

Movies are released each month involving people who struggle for love, money, fame, glory – whatever – you name it. We peek into the lives and adventures of others and watch them struggle, hoping they will find happiness. In the make believe world, boy meets girl and they ride happily off into the sunset. Perfect ending to an imagined story. Rarely are the heroes in our lives so clean cut and victorious. Rarely do we feel that the good guys win over the bad guys. Rarely does the struggle seem worth it in real life. Yet, we continue, hoping and wishing that we one day, we will win in this struggle and our story would have that happy ending.

Why does life have to be about struggle? What is it about us that insist struggle is essential? The answer lies in our belief that we are separate from God, Infinity. After the creator-god convinced us we were separate from God, the i-god convinced us we had a personal separate identity. If you have followed me, you see we now believe we are not one with God, but two or more. We have God. We have me. We have you.

Now, what happens when we have two or more? There is a constant struggle to get something we think we don't have or to keep from losing something we think we do have. We have opponents or opposing forces. Do we want to be right or wrong, strong or weak, a loser or a winner?

Our life stories can now be written and acted out. We have characters, and importantly, we have opposing sides that want different things. The movie of life can now begin! To make the drama complete, my side has to resist the opposing side or other point of view. Why? Because central to the struggle is drama and key to drama is conflict. Now we have all the ingredients. We have separate forces that are in opposition and one force must resist the other.

Unbeknownst to us, is the principle that the more we resist the opposing side or force in our struggle, the more it will persist. Its very existence is dependent upon us making it real, and we do this by opposing it. Good cannot exist without evil. Right must have wrong. Strong cannot be strong without weakness. The mind and its i-god keep this principle far from of our awareness and, we operate as if one force is independent of the other – that good exists without evil, that strength is wholly without weakness. We are taught and expected to struggle against the opposing force, with the ultimate goal of defeating it.

For example, a sixty-year-old man was referred to me. A large corporation had employed him for over 30 years. He was six months short of retirement when he was fired. He was shocked because he was a loyal employee who had never missed a day of work in over 30 years. He would even arrive at least a half hour early everyday to get ahead in his job. He also considered himself a good husband and father. He had never had an affair in over 35 years of marriage and was always there for his children. In short, he was really a "good man" who tried to live a moral life.

Yet, here he was at the end of his career and a great injustice had been done to him. He was so angry that he wanted to kill the new supervisors who were brought in to "shake up" the company by getting rid of what they termed "old baggage." As his anger increased, his wife insisted he seek help.

In our first few sessions, he related that primarily his mother and grandmother raised him. His father was a heavy drinker and left his family for the "street life." After that, he had no contact with his father. The constant message that he received from his mother and grandmother was, he was not to be like his father. As long as he was a good and responsible person he would receive mama's and grandmother's love and approval.

The theme of his life was to reject the bad, his father, and choose the good. This guide had worked for him until he was fired. He began to drink and was obsessed with thoughts of killing his supervisor. These thoughts frightened him for he saw himself as a good Christian and God fearing man. Never could he have conceived of winding up with such thoughts and acting irresponsibly.

He seemed startled when I pointed out he was now acting like his father – something he had been trained to reject and resist. Truly, what he had resisted persisted!   To end his struggle, I told him that he would have to accept his father – accept all that his father had done, without judgment, condemnation, or reservation. In other words, he had to love his father because love cannot be incomplete.

Love is whole, and whatever is resisted is being withheld from love. True love does not rely upon opposition. It knows no opposite! True love or God cannot have an opposite, because it is All. True love or God can only be One. True love means we have no personal identities and must end our struggles by embracing our opposite. Our mind does not want this to happen, for it would no longer have a reason to exist. Its very existence depends on separation, struggle and conflict.

We would rather have stories of pain and struggle than true love because we cling to our separate identities. We believe we are our stories, our experiences, and our struggles. We create drama, action, and problems to perpetuate the basic premise of the creator-god and i-god. We will be separate, struggle and have opposition. That's our story and that is our lives, and we will not give it up.

We think our stories matter, that they are important. The Truth, is they don't matter. They serve only to perpetuate struggle, pain and suffering, not the real live story of Infinite Love, Infinite Truth, Infinite Oneness, which is written off by the script writers of the mind.

We actually trade in all that is beautiful, all that is lovely, all that is peaceful for our stories of struggle and suffering. Now, doesn't this sound stupid and insane? Of course it does, but it makes for an interesting story. Quite interesting. Quite an interesting script as written by the creator- and i-gods. Yet, the story doesn't end here. To make it even more real, the i-god creates another component. Let's see what can be next.

The I God

VIII. Commandment

You will see the solution to your problems as external to yourself.

Recently I was watching television and instead of focusing on the programs, I decided to pay close attention to the commercials. It became apparent to me that the purpose of advertisement was to create a desire or problem for the viewers and convince them that the product being advertised was the solution. As I thought about this scenario, I realized that this not only applies to advertising but also to the basic structure of human life.

Life appears to present us with problems. We have money problems, relationship problems, job problems; you name it. There is never a shortage of problems. The funny thing about it is, almost all of our problems appear to be outside of us. Rarely, do we feel we are the problem. No, it is clear to us. The problem is simple. If it is a money problem, it is because there isn't enough money in our bank account. If it is relationship problem, it is because the other person is not acting right. And, so the story goes. Yet, once the problem is framed as being outside of us, the solution to the problem would naturally also be outside.

This is the way the false gods would have us think. The creator-god initiated this formula and it was passed down through the we-god and onto the i-god, which personally thinks that problems are inherently contained outside of the I that I think I am. Just consider, we were taught in the Book of Genesis, the creator-god had a problem when Adam and Eve ate from the forbidden tree. The creator-god believed the root of the problem was outside of him and he blamed Adam, who blamed Eve, who blamed the snake. A lot of finger pointing to prove that the problem was outside. This scenario is so normal to our way of life that it seems unquestionably true. The problem and the solution are always outside.

I always felt as if something was missing within me – as if I had a big psychological hole, which I dare not let anyone see. As mentioned previously, I tried to cover the hole up by engaging in countless activities culminating in pursuing my Ph.D. degree from an Ivy League school, which I thought would make me feel more complete and respected. "Watch out world, here I come," was what I often said to myself. I felt that after I had completed my requirements for my doctorate, I would set the world on fire. The formula was set for me.

Although I felt bad inside, it was not my fault. I blamed my father for not spending enough time with me. Although I felt unloved, I had the cure. I would remedy that by my academic achievements. Or, so I thought. Once I received my Ph.D., I was surprised to find that the world did not bend over backwards for me – not much changed, especially inside of me. As a result, I descended into the most depressing period of my life, not understanding the causes or dynamics. I was sure I had played the game right. I had earned my degree. I had done what the we-god and i-god commanded, but I still felt empty inside. The hole had not been filled. Little did I know, the scenario was set up by the i-god and we-god to trick me into thinking that satisfaction and completion resided outside of me.

Why didn't I know this, I was a psychologist and knew about the ego-defense mechanisms of repression and projection – two devices Sigmund Freud identified that the ego or i-god uses in self-defense. Repression is simply not allowing threatening or uncomfortable thoughts into awareness, and projection is placing unwanted thoughts and feelings outside of oneself, usually onto another person or situation. I knew about these mechanisms, but didn't think they were at play in my life.

The trickery of the false gods is so cunning and insidious that most of us are not aware of how easily we get sucked into thinking the problem is outside us. I thought I felt empty and inadequate because my father had not spent enough time with me. My problem was a problem, not because of me, but because of my father. He was the one responsible. I thought the solution was to go outside of myself and get degrees and awards that would get me the approval of the we-god. I thought this would make me feel whole. And yet, I never felt whole or complete.

In fact, the problem kept perpetuating itself until one Father's Day when I appeared on a television show with my older son. He was asked what he disliked most about me. Without a second thought, he said he felt cheated because I had not spent enough time with him! Bingo! What goes around comes around. The false gods will not let you out of your psychological prison. I was blaming my father for not spending enough time with me and now my son was blaming me. I was passing on to my son my own misconceptions.

The problem is outside and thus the solution is also outside. Projection works. Freud was right or so it seemed. I knew then and there that the mind had to be confronted on all levels. I knew then that the solution could never be obtained by going outside of oneself. The solution to any problem – money, relationship, job, race, international politics, war, whatever – is always within me.

I realize this may sound insane to some, but the problem, no matter what it is, is always experienced within. Your discomfort or stress always comes from within. The conditions outside will be what they are. Those conditions or situations are just conditions or situations. The uncomfortable feelings are not in the situations or conditions. The discomfort resides within, and no matter where we go, there we are with our feelings and stresses. The i-god will ensure that we will always experience stress, for its job is to create stress. Peace only comes from the Infinite One!

Our job is to go within. Our job is to search inside our psychological structures and see how we are projecting our feelings of inadequacy, guilt and fear onto another person, place or situation. Once we begin this process, we begin to access true peace, for peace is always available. That peace from the Omnipresent God can be brought to our minds, our situations and our circumstances.

How do we do this? We take responsibility for our circumstances or situations. Responsibility does not mean guilt. Responsibility means to be the source of. We begin to see that we are responsible for our feelings. Other people may do things but usually not to intentionally hurt us.

My father didn't intentionally hurt me. He was just busy being a provider. Once I realized this, I relinquished my feelings of resentment towards him and grasped that I was the source of my feelings of resentment. Even in situations where individuals may intentionally try to hurt us, we can also be responsible and comprehend those individuals mistakenly believe that the root of their problem lies outside of them. Eventually, they will hurt themselves more than they hurt us.

Instead of responding with defensiveness, we can have compassion for them because they are stuck in the i-god and creator-god system. This must have been what Jesus thought on the cross when he said, "Father, forgive them for they know not what they do." Jesus' persecutors did not know he was innocent. Rather, they felt guilty, inadequate, and fearful and projected these feelings onto Jesus and made Him wrong. They did not understand the nature of their minds. They did not know what they were doing. They needed forgiveness. They needed compassion.

Normally we do not think this way or forgive when we think the problem and the solution are outside of us. By projecting outside self, we clearly are not loving ourselves or others. We are too busy blaming. We are just frightened little beings keeping the story of the false gods alive. As a result, we are the ones who are trapped in the story. We are the ones who are hurting.

We plod on through our lives not knowing that we are looking for love, success and happiness in all the wrong places. If only we would look inside, past the barriers that the psychological gods have erected, we would find that wonderful and beautiful part of us that is all love, that is all beauty, that is all peaceful. And it is here, right inside of us, but we won't let ourselves see it.

Quite a trick by the i-god and its companions, right? Well, let's see how these false gods continue to trick us in the ninth commandment.

The I God

IX. Commandment

You will engage in meaningless activity believing it has value and purpose.

During my adult life, I have attended many parties, engaged in the required cocktail chit-chat and social niceties. At a recent party, I recall listening to conversations about the social and sexual lives of people around town, a hot stock market tip, ways to make more money, frustrations with spouses or jobs, and so on. As I listened, I found myself participating and realized how bland and meaningless it felt. They were conversations to fill up the space and silence. Silence is often seen as an enemy to be avoided at all cost. So, we talk to break the silence.

As I thought more about it, I realized most of us fill our lives with activities to keep away the silence. Silence, to most of us, looks like death. So, we talk. We get busy. We seek entertainment. We seek relationships. We chase dollars. Anything to not be still and listen. We turn outward seeking things we hope will satisfy us. We set goals to give our lives a purpose. The world outside is always beckoning us to it. So, off we go into the world seeking fortune, fame, satisfaction, our piece of the pie.

We buy books on how to get rich, join investment clubs and attend churches that teach us how to do God's Will, which we think will give us blessings and prosperity. All of these activities seem right and proper, particularly, if they are associated with righteous living.

What's wrong with that, especially if the motive is not greed, but to be a better provider for one's family or to be a more religious person? The answer of course is, nothing. You can do whatever you desire to do. It's all okay. However, the human mind or i-god is so tricky and cunning that we can get caught up in this chase – often finding ourselves depressed or psychologically trapped.

To illustrate, I began to see a forty-five year-old physician in therapy. He complained of depression. He stated that he was at the end of his rope and was so financially in debt that he was considering suicide. He had become a physician because he thought he wanted to help people and could earn a very comfortable income. He ran a string of out-patient clinics throughout the state but had difficulty making payroll. In addition, he had hired several family members, including his brother who he placed in charge of the day-to-day operations of his clinics.

He assumed he could provide assistance to his siblings, while also making "good money." However, his siblings lacked good business sense and he began to lose money, quickly getting into debt. He knew he had to fire his family members but was reluctant to do so. He was the oldest and his mother made him promise before she died that he would be the head of the family.

After several sessions, he was able to see the trap he had put himself in. He fired his relatives and restructured his business. As therapy proceeded, I often asked him, "What's your relationship with money? What purpose does it serve for you?" He was bright and glib and could easily give me surface answers, but when I pressed harder, he was forced to admit that money kept him constantly experiencing lack and struggle. Money was not just money; it was a psychological structure to perpetuate his view of himself and his story about life.

He could never be rich, even if he had millions. He would always feel lack because his core belief about himself was he was lacking and had to struggle. Money was just a symbol. It took awhile for this to sink in. He had to go inside, be still, look within, and tell himself the Truth. Eventually, he was able to change the way he looked at money and what it represented. He was able to experience the freedom he desired. But, is my client unique? Of course not.

This is not just his issue. It is an issue that we all must face. Life is full of symbols, none of which have any inherent meaning or value in and of itself. A two-month old baby has no idea what the value of a hundred dollar bill is. He has to be taught it's value. Once he is taught, he must see that it is only a symbol. A symbol is not real in and of itself. It always represents something. In the case of money, it usually represents abundance, lack, freedom or confinement. Yet, it is still a symbol. We give it meaning. We give it purpose. We give it value by the purpose we assign to it.

If we follow the commandments of the i-god, we will engage in activities that will make the acquisition of the symbol the end goal. Our energy, our life and our strategies will be about acquiring more money. We can justify it, but unless we examine our underlying psychological motives and listen to the still small voice within, all our activities will eventually be meaningless and valueless. History, and I mean recent history, has too many examples of rich people who are unhappy, never knowing it because their activities had little or no meaning or purpose. They were tricked by the i-god and did not know they needed to stop and listen to what is real and true.

To have true meaning and purpose in life, one must be clear that all of life is symbolic. Nothing in this visible or physical world has any true meaning or purpose. We really don't know what is meaningful or valuable because we listen to the voice of the mind. It can only tell us about the valueless. We wind up valuing the valueless. Only the eternal, the invisible, the changeless can bring meaning to life – for it is life! It is total. It is All. It is Infinite. It is real.

What of this physical world that seems so real? What does one do with that? Good questions. The answers lie in the purpose that we give the objects or symbols of the physical world. Unless we use the symbols of the physical world to uncover the psychological barriers that prevent us from knowing that only Spirit is real, we will live in a world of struggle that has little or no meaning. It is similar to Jesus teaching us that we should seek the kingdom of heaven first and then all will be added. And the "all that will be added" is True Love and True Joy.

If there is a purpose in life, perhaps it is realizing that the only goal is for us to know what is real and unchanging. If it does not, then life surely must be without meaning or purpose. How do I know this to be the Truth? This I cannot answer. But, I can say that the i-god and its companions have no desire for you or I to know the Truth. So, let's get the final commandment and see how these false psychological gods attempt to distort the Truth.

The I God

X. Commandment

You will never know the Truth.

Here we are dear reader, we have reached the last of the 30 commandments of the three gods of the mind. And, it is altogether fitting and proper that the final commandment is about Truth – for everything must eventually return to face Truth. Why? Because Truth, God, the Infinite One is all that there is! Therefore God, the Infinite One must be Truth. Anything other than Truth and hence God, is a lie. There cannot be half Truths, as there is no half God! There cannot be my Truth, your Truth and someone else's Truth because Truth is One. It is indivisible. It is All that there is.

Perhaps, this sounds preposterous, since the world shows us events, people, circumstances that can't be true. Lies appear to exist, or that which isn't of God or Truth, in this world. To prove this, you only need to look at the morning paper or look at your own life to see something that isn't of God. And, that's the Truth! Or, so it seems.

That's how it seems to me, to you, and to six billion other people in the world. Six billion people can't be living a lie or can we? How can this be? It just doesn't compute that Truth is all there is and only God or Truth is real. Of course it can't compute to our minds, because they are the sole products of the three gods that we have been discussing. These three gods are able to construct an apparent reality simply because we believe that their commandments are true. We believe that all 30 of the commandments are not only true, but also real. We believe that they operate in the world that we see, believe and know to be real.

We see it, touch it, feel it, think it, and then come to the conclusion that the world outside of us is separate and real. Not only do we believe the world that is separate from us is real, but we believe that we are separate from God or Truth. We make a truth separate from God – a truth that is separate from an indivisible, whole and complete Truth. How insane is that? Very – in fact it is the most insane thought that could ever be phantom, but it is what we believe to be true.

We think it is real because we believe we "know the Truth" and listen to the dictates of the mind – the most insane mechanism that was ever devised. And I, as a clinical psychologist, have a Ph.D. in promoting this insane mechanism! I was taught this in school and am perceived by the world as having expertise in seeing into insanity when in fact, my expertise has been in perpetuating the insane mechanism that separates itself from Truth, beauty, and love.

I realize what I have said so far may be difficult for some of you to accept. So, allow me to give you an example of how the insanity of the human mind operates in terms that may be clearer.

A fifty-year-old African-American male came to see me in therapy. He was by profession a social worker and had achieved a high degree of success in his field. He sought therapy because he was feeling agitated and depressed. He was engaged to an African-American woman, but was constantly fighting with her regarding a past relationship she had. She revealed to him, one night after sexual intimacy, that while she was in her first marriage, she had an affair with a White male, and stated that she had experienced the greatest sex ever with her White companion.

My client became enraged and began to accuse her of adultery and wanted to know how she could not only betray her African-American husband, but how she could have sex with what he described as a White racist? He felt ashamed for attacking her and realized that her past was her past. Even worse, he was experiencing great conflict because he had marched with Dr. King in the 1960's and believed in racial integration and equality. Yet, he was angry with her and felt he had to prove that he was a better lover than her former White lover.

He stated that he realized the insanity of his predicament but felt unable to extract his feelings and constant thoughts of her making love to what he constantly referred to as a White racist. As we discussed his feelings of competition with her former lover, he revealed that he had grown up in a small town in Mississippi and had watched the Klu Klux Klan ride by his house. He also referred to the constant indignities his father endured at the hands of White racists in his hometown. He blamed his father's early death on the depression and pain his father experienced at the hands of racist.

Although I had compassion and sensitivity for my client, I also saw how he was caught in the insanity of the mind. Even though the affair had occurred prior to his relationship with his fiancé, his mind had shaped it so he experienced the affair as if it was in the present. Time was for him not an actual event; it was a psychological experience that fortified his emotional prison.

His feelings of inadequacy were too much for him to handle; so, he projected them outward onto his fiancé, blaming her for his condition. She was guilty, White people were guilty, but not him.

He was unhappy and felt trapped because he really loved his fiancé and did not want to leave her. I pointed out to him that it really did not matter ultimately if he left her or not. The issue was really about his guilt and his inadequacy and no matter where he went or whom he was with, he would carry those feelings with him. The relationship was an opportunity for him to become aware of his hidden guilt and insecurities and heal them, which would allow him the opportunity to be whole and truly love himself and her. And, what else was there for him to do than to learn how to truly love?

He was able to see this and began to work on healing the wounds that were still painful. However to heal, he had to accept that the source of the pain was not outside of him but inside. The pain was the mind that constantly told him that others were wrong and hence guilty; that his fiancé was wrong and hence guilty; that the White lover was wrong and hence guilty; that White people in general were wrong and hence guilty; that the world was wrong and hence guilty.

He had to see the reverse of these. He had to begin to see that this guilt resided within him; it was not outside of himself. His fiancée did what she did, but she was not inherently guilty. He judged her as guilty out of his mind's need to see guilt. Someone must be wrong. Someone has to be blamed. Someone must be punished.

That seems to be the Truth. Sure it does. It is the story of life. Just think about it. Somewhere in our lives, we had an experience where someone did us wrong and we believe they are guilty and deserve to be punished. Black people think White people are wrong and hence, guilty. White people think Black people are wrong or inferior and hence, guilty. Jews think Palestinians are wrong and hence, guilty. Palestinians think Jews are wrong and hence, guilty. It is the story of life simply because, it is the story put forth by the mind as true.

It seems true because it feels true and almost everyone will agree that someone is wrong and hence, guilty. Even the god in Genesis thought Adam and Eve were wrong and hence, guilty. It is the Truth. You can't convince the world or me otherwise. Who or what else is telling us this is the Truth? Where else can we be getting these ideas or thoughts from other than our minds? Where else? Nowhere else if we would get really honest. Nowhere else.

It is the mind – the three mental gods with their commandments that pronounce so loudly that they can tell us what is true. But, how can they? The three gods of the mind are caught in a time/space dimension that can only define reality to a certain time and a certain space. Within the three dimensions the mind can make the past seem so real and so true that it becomes the present. My client felt that his fiancé's past was present.

Time is controlled and experienced by the mind. In fact, the universal mind has to make time seem so real and so true that we can't think outside of it. Yet, eternity or Infinity is outside of time. Eternity is not a long time. Eternity is infinite and thus, immeasurable, simply **because** it is Infinite. Eternity eliminates time. The two cannot co-exist. One eliminates the other!

Eternity or Infinity must therefore be because it is all there is. Therefore it is the Truth – the Truth that the mind cannot know of. It is what I think Jesus spoke of when he said, "My

Kingdom isn't of this world." Truth is beyond the world of the physical or mental. It is the world of the invisible. It is Spirit. It is pure and whole. It is beyond anything the mind can conceive, simply because it is beyond any concept. It cannot be contained by a thought or idea. It is Infinite. It is One. It is truly the I that is. It is the only I that is. It is the I Am that I am and that "I" is our identity. I and the Father or Truth are One. And, that's the Truth!!

PART III

THE WAY
OUT

Chapter 11

Introduction to the Way Out

The Way Out

Dear reader, we have traveled a great distance on this journey. We have undertaken the greatest journey of all - exploring our minds to look at our lives from a different perspective. What we have discovered so far is there is only one Mind, and that is the Mind of God. This Mind is Infinite and unknowable to our finite minds. We have found a way to make something happen that we never before would have thought possible.

We think we were able to split off from the One Mind, and another mind that considered itself separate and distinct came to be. This separate mind appears to be universal. It appears to have power in and of itself, and with that power it created other finite minds. They too accepted the basic belief that they were separate and distinct. Out of this came a belief in separation.

Besides individual minds, we explored the even greater power of the collective mind, also called the group mind. The collective mind is composed of separate and distinct minds that appear to be the reality of who we are and the way the world is.

All the problems, the chaos, the trouble, and suffering of the world have come from this basic principle of separation.

From this evolved what we call history. History is the past and lays the basis for what we believe to be the future. This belief in separation has created all that we have known. From this belief has come, what I conclude is, you and me.

The problem is I believe I am a finite identity separated from other finite identities. In other words, my only problem is that I am identified as an individual human with a finite form called a body. I must see other limited forms that are contained within bodies as separate forms. Once this premise is accepted as the basis of our identity the three gods become real, because their commandments appear to be true.

All of this is simply because we don't question the basis of who we are. When we question the true nature of our identity, the collective universal mind resists and fights to retain its allegiance to the principle of separation. It will do anything, in its supposed power, to ensure we do not find our true identity, which is Infinite Love.

Most of us do not operate from the premise that we are Infinite Love. If we did, there would be no need for this book. We would not need to be reminded that we are Love, and Loved in an unconditional and unalterable state.

One day we will all recognize the Truth about our identity, but that day has not yet arrived. As a result, I, a human who is also apparently caught up in the psychological web of human thought and conditioning of the three gods, will attempt to offer ways we can escape the psychological maze that keeps us from our true identity. I say, I will offer it to you, simply to emphasize the basic spiritual principle: If I truly want to learn something, I must teach it and then I can get it. It is akin to the age-old saying, "If you really want to keep something, you must give it away." This affirms the principle that you can't give what you don't have.

It is only at the level of human thinking that we believe there are matters that we don't know. At our deepest spiritual level however, we know all there is to know. The next section of this book will address that level of our psychological mind. We will address methods to get untangled from the psychological web about the ignorance of our true identity.

In the previous section, three psychological gods with their ten commandments were identified. By obeying these commandments, we experience pain and suffering. Infinite love, on the other hand, does not offer pain and suffering. It can only be. It does not judge, punish, or attack. It only accepts.

I propose ten acceptances rather than commandments. The acceptances will show us the light of the true knowledge of ourselves. These ten acceptances, when fully recognized and practiced, offer us ten corresponding gifts to discover our true worth. With this in mind, let's embark on the next phase of our journey. As we learn how to escape the psychological prison of our mind, we will experience the power of accepting our true identity.

Chapter 12

The Ten Acceptances
And Their Gifts

The Ten Acceptances And Their Gifts

I.   Go within to get out. The gift is guidance.

II. Uncover your psychological mechanisms. The gift is knowledge of your psychological identity.

III. Surrender to your attachments and release yourself. The gift is freedom.

IV. Relinquish guilt and fear that keep you from joining. The gift is true joining.

V.   Know that all relationships can point to Oneness or Love. The gift is to see all as One.

VI. Be willing to question what you think is real. The gift is the knowledge of that which is Truly Real.

VII. Stay in the now. The gift is eternal peace and understanding.

VIII. Know that the invisible is what is Real. The gift is wisdom.

IX. Be willing to view death differently. The gift is a new birth.

X.   Know that your true identity is spirit. The gift is knowing you are Christ or Unconditional Love.

I. Acceptance

Go Within To Get Out

While pondering how to introduce the concept of escaping the hell inside our minds, I saw the intricate and diabolical way the universal mind has set up things to keep us hostage. The mind, in its cleverness, has devised a simple but most effective way to ensure we stay stuck in our misery. It tells us the problem and solution is outside of us. Sounds simple and, it is. It's so simple that it is brilliant in its diabolical nature. By saying the solution to our problem is outside of us, it ensures we will never get to the source of the problem, which is always within.

It is like my car being broken, and going to the kitchen, repairing the refrigerator as though it will repair the car. It doesn't take a rocket scientist to figure out that this wouldn't work. Indeed, if I made repairs to the refrigerator and expected the repairs to magically take care of the car, you would probably call me crazy, or even stupid. And, you would be right. Yet, this is the principle most of the world uses to solve problems.

We have a tendency to look at everything except the source for the solution of the problem. We look outside ourselves, at our neighbors, our spouse, our enemy – those other folks, be they White people, Black people, women, men, Moslems, Christians, Palestinians, Jews, Iraqi, even the devil. You name it. It's just not us! I'm not the one with the problem. It is you. It is them that are causing our problem. Always them. Never us.

Even when we concede that we contributed to the problem, we don't think we are solely responsible for the mess we're in. Rarely do we search deep within, because that would be a tremendous violation of the commandments of the three gods. They don't want us to discover the Truth. They don't want us to see into their functioning and make-up. Never will they reveal themselves to us as the maker of the mess in our lives. If they did, we would see them for the liars and deceivers they are.

A lie can only exist and have power over you when you refuse to believe it as a lie. The mind and its three gods keep insisting that the problem is out there. As a result, we never see the real problem maker – our minds.

Even traditional psychology does not understand the depth and nature of this mechanism. Traditional psychology believes that minds are separate and personal. It does not know there is one universal thought-based mind. Nor does it know that this universal mind or thought of separation has three little minds, which obey its laws.

Unless this universal mind is addressed, it does no good to fix the separate, individual minds. It is as if General

Motors had a design flaw in its manufacturing plant that produced its cars and the employees attempted to fix each individual car without correcting the flaw in the design. It is this same principle with the mind. We must see that the real flaw lies in the creator of this design, not each individual mind. We must go to the source to have any real impact.

That source is the initial belief or thought that Infinity, God could have something separate from It. It is from that thought alone that all other beliefs arose. The three mental gods and their commandments, the trouble of nations fighting nations, races hating each other, families unable to love one another and individuals hating themselves came from the thought of separation. All the troubles known to mankind stemmed from this one belief. The only way we can deal with this belief is to go within to see it and be willing to release ourselves from it. Otherwise we stay stuck in the human drama of finger-pointing and blaming – the story that has been going on since the beginning of time.

Let me illustrate how we look outside for the source of our problems. I was seeing a couple for marriage counseling. In our sessions each would accuse the other of not meeting their needs. The husband felt neglected because his wife did not agree to regular sexual activities. The solution to his problem was simple, she should agree to more sex.

Obviously his wife had a different perspective. To her, he was always working, or hanging out with his friends, and on top of that, he didn't communicate. She felt unappreciated and neglected. The problem was clear to her. Her husband was not attentive or sensitive to her concerns. The solution was as plain as the nose on her face. Her husband should change and then she would change. Very reasonable. Very clear. Very fair.

From her husband's perspective, his solution was just as clear, reasonable and fair. They saw the problem from their relative perspectives. Neither party was wrong, but they could not agree on a solution. Granted they could work out some temporary ways to reconcile their differences, as traditional psychology could help them do, but no permanent solution or true joining could occur unless the real source of their problems was addressed.

My focus was to help them realize that it was not just a personal or personality issue that separated them. It was an issue that reached into the core of their beings. It was the issue we learned from the creator-god, which states blame is the basic principle in all relationships. Regardless of what they did personally, it was the universal belief that someone had done someone wrong, as stated in the ninth commandment of the i-god, which prevented them from joining as a couple. If they truly wanted a loving relationship, they would have to understand that the source of their problem was not only personal, residing within the i-god of their respective minds, but was also societal from the we-god and was inherently implanted within them like DNA.

The only way they could escape from this DNA - like problem was to go within and examine every belief of the three mental gods. They had to see that the gods within prevented them from knowing and experiencing the true power of joining.

In each session they began to examine the beliefs of each mental god and saw how they affected their lives and distorted the Truth about themselves and each other. By examining themselves at a deep psychological and spiritual level, they began to emerge from the hell-hole that the mind had put them in.

This, dear reader, was not only true for them but is for us all. To get out, we must go within. There is no other way. It is the point that I think Jesus was making when he said, "The Kingdom of Heaven lies within." Only within . . . Never without. Within all of us is the answer – the solution. Ultimately, we must know that there is no without and nothing is outside of the awareness of who we really are. There is only One Mind, and that Mind is the Mind of God or Infinity.

Although my married couple was not fully aware of this Truth, eventually, they, like all of us, will come to this. Until then, we must keep asking questions that will direct us inward. The gift we get from doing this is true guidance, true direction to that place of Infinite Love and acceptance. The Guide that is within all of us gives this gift of guidance.

It is a Guide that knows the true way out, for It has never been and can never be caught up by the three gods in our minds – for It is not mental. It is Spirit. It is beyond the world of the mental. It is always available to us, although seemingly temporarily blocked by our psychological processes and inability to acknowledge Its presence.

It cannot be forever denied or destroyed, because It is eternal and ever-present, waiting on us to ask It to guide us out of the hell of our minds. All we need do is to sincerely ask and It must respond with unconditional love. Quite a gift, as I see it, even if we feel like we don't deserve it. The Internal Guide does not care about such concerns because it knows the games of the mental gods. Freedom is always available and we have begun this journey and taken the first step toward true acceptance.

II. Acceptance

Uncover Your Psychological Mechanisms

Stress! We know what it does to our lives because it is persistent. The more we try to reason with it, or get rid of it, the more it seems to follow us. We take pills, we try a new relationship, change jobs, have an affair, make more money, get a divorce, buy a new house, end romantic relationships, go to church, exercise, remarry, go to therapy, quit therapy, or try yoga. We're always looking for something new to rid our lives of stress. But, it always returns and rears its ugly head.

So, what are we left with? Perhaps, the answer lies in the simple fact that we have not gotten to the underlying source of the stress. Our attempts to rid stress from our lives could be similar to getting rid of an ugly tree by cutting off the branches instead of digging up the roots.

What is the root of our stress? It has to be our minds. If they weren't the culprits how would we know we were experiencing stress? What tells us that we are experiencing stress? Our i-god informs us. Our i-god tells us how to identify and react to stress. But, beware of a trick. The i-god, or your personal mind, never reveals its own will, the real nature of the way it produces stress and how to get rid of it.

In fact, it invariably will say the source of the stress is outside of you, as noted in the prior acceptance.

It is just about always the other guy who is the cause of your stress. It's never you. It's your neighbor, spouse, boss, co-worker, White people, Black people, anybody. They're at fault. They are the cause.

Even when we admit the source of our stress is within, rarely do we understand the true nature of the mechanism that causes us so much worry. For it is the nature of the mind, with its three gods, to conceal its real intention from us. It tells us what is wrong with the world, what's wrong with other people, and ourselves.

The real purpose of the mind is to keep us forever anxious and insecure. It tells us that we are worried and unhappy because others have done us wrong. It makes us believe the only way we can relieve ourselves of these bad feelings is to attack the wrongdoers. It secretly desires that we remain stuck so it can rule supreme and have us in constant worry and anxiety - the very foundation of the three false gods.

What if we understood these psychological mechanisms? It would be like taking an axe and chopping away the root of the psychological mechanism that keeps us caught in misery. It is a critical step in freeing ourselves from the hell of our minds. I imagine some of you are asking, "Tell me more. What is my mechanism? How can I get out?" The best way I can respond to these excellent questions is to describe interactions with a patient who had similar questions.

A few years ago, a forty something year old African-American female came to see me after her second divorce. Although she had reached a high level in the corporate world, she was having difficulty sleeping and felt a sense of emptiness. She stated that she knew she wasn't "crazy", but she just didn't quite know who she was and how to find happiness in life.

She was raised in a fairly religious home, had converted to Catholicism and felt somewhat guilty about her divorces, particularly her first one. Additionally, her two children were in college. She felt that they had survived the break-up of the family fairly well, primarily because of her attempt to shelter them from the pain of such a separation. So, why was she feeling so upset and anxious? To get to the heart of the question, I know the answer lies in the core belief that we have about ourselves.

It lies in the core belief that we have about ourselves – that something is wrong with us – something so terrible that we dare not look at it. Theologically, it is equated with knowing that at our core we are sinful, having committed the unthinkable act against all that is good, all that is perfect, all that is wonderful – sinned against God. This core belief is the bedrock for all minds. It is the basis for the creator-god. However, as individuals, we identify personally through the dictates of the i-god or personal mind.

My patient's core belief was she was not good enough. As a young child, she never knew that her father loved her. He was very critical and controlling, always expecting her to achieve and be a "good girl", and she did. Fortunately, she was intellectually gifted and achieved in school. She always brought home excellent report cards. Also, she vowed to remain a virgin until she married, eliminating her risk of becoming pregnant and incurring her father's punishment and rejection. Her drive for success and moral rightness was, in reality, a cover for her feelings of inadequacy and insecurity.

In therapy, she was able see that she was so afraid of others discovering that she was not good enough. She worked extremely hard in school and later at her profession to show that she was indeed worthy and adequate. She became successful and graduated Summa Cum Laude in college and took a job in corporate America rising quickly up the ranks. After all, she was bright, witty, attractive, and hard working.

In her first marriage, she juggled being a good wife and mother with a career. She thought she was doing a good job until she discovered that her husband was having an affair and wanted to leave. The pain was terrific and she fought diligently to save her marriage but was unsuccessful. To numb the pain of failure and her core feelings of inadequacy, she remarried a few months after her divorce and tried to get back on track by being successful the second time around.

Remember, the mind has an intention to keep our core beliefs alive and active. My patient had a core belief that she was inadequate and felt insecure **despite** her professional success. Quite predictably, her second marriage ended after two years. Her core beliefs had emerged supreme. She now knew she was not good enough. She now knew she was inadequate. No promotion or salary increases could drown out the loud screams from her personal mind or i-god.

As we discussed her predicament in therapy, I pointed out that our lives are fairly predictable and if closely examined, we would discover that they are not that random. It is as if our lives are on railroad tracks and those tracks are our core beliefs that take us to a destination called worry and anxiety. With some discussion, after I requested her to write an autobiography, she began to identify not only the core beliefs but also the main junctures along her life path that showed the workings of those beliefs.

To deepen her awareness, I instructed her to set aside one day to simply observe and write down how her mind worked by watching her thoughts and judgments, and how she defended herself and attacked others with her thoughts. When she returned to the next session after completing this assignment, she was amazed that she spent most of her day judging others or herself, but primarily others. I informed her that this was the nature of the mind, for we all feel inadequate and inferior. Not wanting to really experience the full brunt of this pain, we project it outward and judge others as inferior or superior. We are always judging.

Judging is the foundation of all our reactions. We are never free to be with others or ourselves because we are always prepared to react. We are robots with little or no ability to respond other than the way our judgments tell us to. We can never truly be with another as long as we function as psychological robots, programmed to interpret the world consistent with our basic beliefs about ourselves and the way we think the world is.

Interpretations, however, can never be facts. They are beliefs or opinions and, hence, not necessarily true. Only Truth is true. Interpretations and their subsequent reactions may offer us temporary relief from our feelings of inadequacy but they will never give us true peace and tranquility. They are mechanisms employed by the three mental gods to keep us feeling inadequate.

As my patient began to accept this premise, she began to acquire a handle on her mechanism. However, more work had to be done. Having a hand on the handle does not necessarily release one from the mechanism. To get release from the psychological mechanism, one must go beyond psychology. One must go beyond the mind. One must, so to speak, go outside of the mind to be free of the mind. For my patient and for all of us this requires that we go into the realm of the Spirit.

As I mentioned earlier, my patient was raised a Protestant but later converted to Catholicism. After her divorces, she began to question her concept of God and felt she was drifting with very little spiritual direction. She knew she could no longer remain in traditional religion, but she didn't know where to go. In therapy, I reassured her it was not only safe to question her religious training, but it was necessary for her to be open to new and varied ways of thinking about God, love and Truth.

We spent hours talking about Religion, God, and Spirituality. It is my basic assumption that growth can only occur when one is willing to look at life differently. When we are willing to view our world and ourselves differently, all possibilities can emerge. This was the door that I persistently pointed her towards, and this was the door that she began to open.

Spiritually, she began to look at nontraditional approaches, trying what she described as metaphysical or New Age methods. Initially she was excited about these approaches. She saw new possibilities for herself, but after some initial good feelings, her old pattern of feeling inadequate returned. Again she covered up her feelings with more professional success and accomplishments. A lack or hunger still existed because she remained within the clutches of her psychological mechanism or i-god.

As long as she identified as a human, she would have those psychological mechanisms. The best she could do was to become aware of them and surrender to a force that was greater than she. In other words, she had to realize that she was essentially impotent in changing her psychological structure. She could be aware of it, identify it, understand it, and observe it, but real power could only come from the One True Power. That Power is Omnipotent and ever present. It is All.

Her recognition, mind and yours, has to be the same recognition that Jesus knew when he said: "Of myself I can do nothing. It is the Father within that does the work." It is the recognition that the universal mind with its three mental gods has no inherent power to make us worry, anxious, and unhappy. What we must do is recognize this as Truth and see these mechanisms for what they are – simply a set of beliefs that deceive us. If we would observe how they function in our lives and surrender ourselves to the Only Power, then and only then will peace – true peace – the peace that passes all understanding emerge.

My patient began to see this and every day and even every conscious moment, she must remind herself of this task and her commitment to it. Although she isn't always successful – she is doing so more frequently and is achieving true success. She is obtaining for herself her true gift - self-knowledge. She is beginning to realize her psychological self is not her true self and is starting to know that her true identity lies in her spiritual awareness.

She has learned that her psychological mechanisms serve as a closet that seemingly hides the brilliance of her True Self. She has learned not to be tricked into believing the three mental gods, which say she is not good enough. She is able to shift the focus of her identity from a psychological source to a Spiritual Source. This is the gift that she is giving herself. This is indeed one of the greatest gifts she can receive. This is also available to you and me if we really want it. All we have to do is go within, watch, notice, observe, and surrender. This sounds simple, yes. Difficult? Yes, but oh so rewarding.

III. Acceptance

Surrender to Your Attachments and Release Yourself

Recently, I visited a friend's house with several other African-Americans. As is common when a group of Black people get together, the issue of race arose. Instead of actively participating as I usually do, I decided to sit back and observe.

The discussion proceeded along a familiar path. Some lamented the state of Black/White relations in the U.S. Most agreed that social conditions had changed since the 1960's and 70's, but racism remained a central focus of American life. Black people lacked the central strong leadership we had with Dr. King and Malcolm X. The conversation continued with little agreement except for the fact that the present state of Black America demanded a new approach to dealing with race relations. The approaches from 30 or 40 years ago were out of date and ineffective.

As I was driving home from my friend's house, I thought about the conversations I had heard. I also thought about a patient of mine named Harold. I had been seeing him for an extended period of time. He initially sought therapy due to mild depression and anxiety problems. He is in his

50's and an African-American who had risen to a responsible position with a large corporation.

During our initial therapy session, Harold said he grew up in a small town in Georgia and attended a historically Black college during the 1960's. While in college he participated in several civil rights demonstrations. In the 1970's, Harold attended a large, prestigious predominantly white university in the Northeast. He earned an M.B.A., and later entered the corporate world.

As he shared his professional and personal history with me, he saw clearly that race played a significant role in his development. He attended a segregated elementary school and high school. So, he enrolled in a historically Black college to be with the "Brothers and Sisters during the civil rights revolution." He maintained that he believed in racial integration, and considered Dr. King a role model and a civil rights leader. Indeed, while a participant in the civil rights movement, Harold began to date White females. He contended he could not become emotionally attached to them, because they could not understand the real struggles of Black people.

He later became involved in the Black consciousness movement of the early 1970's, and changed his mind about integration. He saw where integration hurt Black people. It was during this phase of his life that he was attending a major White university. He contended he had to compete with White males, particularly for grades. He began to think the university was mostly racist, and he only felt comfortable in the company of other Black students.

Harold graduated with an M.B.A., but he was not in the top of his class as he had been in undergraduate school. He said White people had a different approach to the educational system, and his classmates had an unfair advantage over him. But, he was satisfied that he had "made it at the White man's school."

After Harold graduated, he entered the corporate world and, as he stated, "really had to learn how to play the White man's game." He studied the mannerisms of successful White managers, and he quickly developed a strategy for acquiring success. Although Harold knew he was not White and was at an alleged disadvantage, he felt he could overcome it with a combination of hard work, determination and more hard work. And, that he did. Yet, he had an underlying resentment toward the racial unfairness he detected in the system. He dared not openly express his feelings at work, because he feared that he would not be promoted.

Additionally, Harold knew it was important that he maintain his Black consciousness and not "sell out" as he saw some of his other Black colleagues do. In fact, he held great contempt for Black colleagues who had sold out to the White man. He constantly referred to them as "handkerchief-head Negroes." Yet he continued to work hard and "play the game".

Underneath, Harold still felt resentment toward White males who had an unfair advantage over him. His desire to succeed by then was fueled by his desire to prove to White co-workers that he was just as good, or even better than they were. Thus, Harold set out on a path familiar to many African Americans today as the Black middle class expands.

For Harold race was crucial. It played a central role in his life, and became one of the primary lens through which he viewed himself and his world. "And why not?" he often said emphatically. "After all, America is founded on race and the oppression of Black people, and I would be a fool," he contended, "if I thought, or saw it any other way."

I agreed with him to a certain extent. But, as with everything else, I said if he truly wanted to be intelligent and wise he would have to ask other questions - questions that would make him uncomfortable. Questions that would challenge his basic assumptions about himself, his beliefs, and the way he saw the world.

Harold seemed confused by what I said, but he was open to discussions. I told him that everything had a price and there was no free lunch. I said he had to look at the price he was paying, as well as the benefits he was deriving from his position on his race. I said until he was willing to do this he would be dominated by race and unable to act in a free and open manner.

As he considered my point, Harold began to examine his beliefs and his stand on race. Initially, he saw that he derived a clear and safe sense of selfhood from his racial identity, and it offered a degree of security. As I pressed him harder to go deeper within, Harold began to see the sense of security he derived from his racial identity, and realized it covered up his insecurities and fears.

This discovery was initially upsetting to him, because he did not want to admit he was afraid, and he clearly could not admit he was afraid of White people, particularly White males. He stated very proudly that he had "played the White man's game" and beat them at it. He said he proved to the corporate world that Black men can be just as good, or better than White men. He earnestly felt White men were afraid to face the Truth.

I quickly agreed with Harold, and told him that all relationships, including racial ones, are based on fear and that White men are afraid of Black people, and Black men in particular. Otherwise, there would be no reason for them to attack us the way they have and continue to do. However, the flip side of the coin is equally as true. I wanted Harold to learn that Black men have been conditioned by the White-oriented system to feel inferior, and at some level Blacks have accepted it.

The bottom line is both groups are driven by fear but mask it with a racially superficial cover-up. As a result, no truly productive actions or results can occur, because those actions are fear-based and fear-driven. The mind with its three gods has thus created an unsolvable situation between Blacks and Whites, and neither group truly knows who they are. Nor will either group truly achieve happiness or peace.

"What is one to do?" asked Harold. "Are Black people to simply forego our blackness and become handkerchief-head Negroes, always appeasing White people while never complaining? Are we supposed to accept White values, White culture, and the White definition of a good Black person?"

"Of course not," I replied. "But we must be willing to let go of our need to be Black. By this I mean we, as Black people, must begin to understand the role that race or any other belief we have plays, and we must see that our need to identify with any concept will limit us. Our identity is limitless. It is beyond any label, it is beyond any concept of identity. Our identity is spiritual, yet we appear to live in a world where race plays an important role. We must know that only in our minds are we maintaining the position that we are spiritual beings who act and function in a racist world. We are fighting opponents, be they White, Black, Jewish or any other race of people, **in our minds**."

The battle is always within us. The battle must be fought from within and resolved from within before any success can be experienced outside of us. The enemy never changes. It is fear and Blacks and Whites must own it, watch it and observe it. Initially, we may find it difficult not to react, but if we stay committed to knowing our true identity is spiritual, the internal struggle lessens. We will become more effective in dealing with the external world where racism and other negative forces exist. Our motivation will come from a space of inner calm and peace rather than fear and opposition. This inner state of peace will, therefore, control the outer actions and allow for peace. The external can only reflect that which is internal. So, if I am peaceful within, I can have peace without.

As I explained this to Harold, he seemed to be somewhat skeptical and reluctant to accept these points. He said it was a weak position that made him vulnerable, and neither he nor any Black person could afford to be in such a state again with White people. Yet, Harold also realized the traditional ways of dealing with social problems have not been effective, and racial division and hatred continue to be very much a part of American life.

I left him with these points to consider. I also asked him to consider the price he paid individually, and the price we pay, as Black people, to continue our fear-based relationships. I asked him what experiences it would take for him to face his fears in general and his fears of White people in particular?

I questioned if he would consider the idea of surrendering his fears. This was for Harold one of the most difficult moments in our sessions. And to his credit, he admitted it was extremely uncomfortable for him to confront his fears, to embrace them and surrender them.

He gradually began to see that unless he was willing to surrender all his fears, he would continue to be the victim of racism. Soon he was able to talk about his fear of feeling White male coworkers were superior to him. He began to realize that fear was actually a psychological thought that kept him imprisoned within the emotional jail cell of his mind.

Escape was possible by tackling this fear head-on. The process involved observing the fear, then releasing it to a spiritual source by not identifying it as part of his true identity. The gift Harold received from doing this was one that he now says he wanted all along for himself and his people. The gift is the gift of freedom. It is a freedom that not only Dr. King and Malcolm X had died for, but a freedom that Jesus also apparently died for.

It is the freedom that liberates. It allows us to be who we truly are. It goes beyond the confines of the mind to a place where there are no limitations or boundaries. That is what freedom is, and it awaits us all. It is here now if we will just let go of our minds and surrender to the One and All Infinite Spiritual Source.

IV. Acceptance

Relinquish Guilt and Fear That Keep You From Joining

As Harold and I continued to see each other, I saw him struggling with the new ideas that were evolving in our sessions. I marveled at the manner in which he would engage himself and struggle as he questioned the most basic assumptions and beliefs about his life. At times, Harold acted like an excited child on Christmas morning. At other times, he showed contempt for me and toward anything that made him feel uncomfortable or threatened. Yet, he persisted.

He said it was an exciting journey he had undertaken, and he felt he had come too far to turn around. And, indeed, he had. He had jumped off the cliff of indecisiveness, and was falling toward a welcome mat of self-discovery. Harold agreed with my assessment, but had to let me know he wasn't always comfortable with the ideas that were presented to him. I complemented him on his honesty, and reassured him that the initial phase of the self-discovery journey was quite upsetting to the universal mind with its three mental gods. They are threatened by this process, realizing that their commandments may no longer be seen as commandments, but as false beliefs set forth to perpetuate a state of depression and anxiety – the very conditions that caused Harold to seek therapy.

As we continued with our sessions, Harold would ask plenty of questions, and would usually let me know at the beginning of each session that he had some reservation about what he was experiencing. He would start many sessions with a cynical but friendly remark such as, "Well, Doc, what revelations do you have from the mountain top today?"

I would laugh and tell him I had not been to the mountaintop but, instead, my feet were wet from walking on water. Once we had gone through our preliminary positioning, Harold said he was having reservations about surrendering his fears. He felt that if he surrendered his fear of White men and if he allowed himself to feel inferior to them, then White men would win and that would be intolerable.

I told him I could understand his position because I also had experienced this. I explained his feelings were only the mind's way of keeping us in conflict, misery and the belief that life is a win-lose situation. Life is structured by the creator-god in a way that someone must win, which means someone else must lose. In fact, losing for some of us is associated with such an intense fear that it seems like death. When I said this, Harold agreed and exclaimed, "See doc, don't you understand why I can't let go entirely? I would lose too much."

I asked him to look at this issue a little deeper and see if he could see anything differently. I explained that he was being driven by an emotional response that kept him enmeshed in a struggle that would cause more pain and suffering unless he was willing to examine his beliefs.

As Harold looked deeper into this issue, he saw that his fear of loss had a tremendous hold on him. Not only was he afraid of losing to White men, he was afraid of many potential losses, such as the loss of his job, respect, family and, of course the big one, his life. Loss and fear controlled his life. Fear was his constant companion, whether he was aware of it or not. Fear makes sure happiness does not exist in one's life. It slams the door in the face of happiness!

Harold began to see the role fear played in his life, and the high price he paid to have it around. He began to realize that release from fear was essential to his emotional well-being. Ignoring, avoiding, and fighting his fear of White men only gave them power over him, a power he was afraid they eventually would garner anyway. He had to find a way to embrace his fear. This would help him acquire the power from within to alter and eventually eliminate it. Fear cannot exist with love. The two are like day and night. Where one is the other cannot be. Where love is, true power is also. That's what I repeated to Harold, but he admitted he didn't understand the connection between fear, power and love.

"Most of us don't. The main reason there are so many problems in the world today is our inability to see our lives and the lives of others differently," I explained.

As Harold addressed his fear and realized how much it controlled his life, he shared that fear wasn't the only thing that affected him. He spent a lot of time looking at a world that he said was unfair. In this unfair world, rich White people control the vast resources. Oppressed people wind up with little or nothing.

"The poor never win," he said. "And those in control, those who possess power over the oppressed, must be held accountable for their greed and their oppressive positions."

I knew what Harold was referring to, but I also knew how the mind structures our lives, whether we are rich or poor. We are structured to suffer. The rich may have more clout and material possessions, but unless they know about the mind and true riches, they are also oppressed. So, I began a series of discussions with Harold to help him see this situation differently.

If he thought rich and greedy people were the cause of the social condition of the poor and oppressed people in the world, he had now introduced another psychological component into the picture that was equally as strong as fear. I called it fear's Siamese twin: guilt.

Guilt and fear are so connected that where one is the other has to be. Guilt and fear were so intimately connected that they essentially share the same purpose, which is to ensure people remain separate. Fear screams the threat of loss. Guilt states that someone is wrong.

Once I felt Harold trusted me enough to not see me as attacking his core beliefs, I explained how the universal mind and the creator-god had set the world up to ensure guilt was present. I told him to think of it this way, the universal mind had a thought it was separate from God and knew it did wrong when it did that. With that one act, guilt was implanted into all our minds and we were born guilty or, as some religions say, "we were born with original sin."

The mind in its cleverness realized the guilt was too intense. So, it devised a way to relieve us of our guilt, by inventing the psychological defense mechanisms of repression and projection. Repression makes us unaware that guilt was designed by the universal mind and perpetrated by the creator god. The defense mechanism of projection aids in this process by placing the guilt outside of us. It makes us see guilt in others, and not in ourselves.

Not only does the creator-god use these mechanisms, but the we-god displays them in instances where one group blames another for its condition. The i-god uses projection and repression when we feel unworthy or wrong. It makes us invest a lot of time and energy seeing others as wrong and hence, guilty.

As I explained these psychological processes to Harold, he was able to see some merit in them, but soon returned to the righteousness of his position and insisted that there were people who were wrong. I reminded Harold that he was on a spiritual journey, and his goal was to be more spiritually conscious and aware. He quoted a scripture where Jesus said, "That which ye do to the least of these, ye do also to me."

I told Harold that Jesus was showing us there are connections, and the word "me" could have meant Jesus or us. In other words, whenever we see someone that we think is guilty, we also see ourselves as being guilty. Projection doesn't work. It only appears to work. Whatever appears to have been cast out from our minds actually stays with us. We don't get rid of guilt by making others guilty. We only think we do.

"It is a trick of the three mental gods," I said to Harold. "It is a paradox. The human mind uses guilt and fear to make us believe we are separate from others. The Truth is: these mechanisms of the mind connect us in unhealthy ways, which result in conflict and anger, guilt's usual companions. White and Black, rich and poor, oppressor and oppressed, even men and women can never truly join in a loving and healthy way as long as guilt is seen in another. Guilt and fear entangle us. Only love joins us."

Harold seemed somewhat confused, but he was engaged. At some level, he was willing to consider these principles, particularly as he was uncovering the diabolical structure of the mind with its three gods. It isn't an easy task to release yourself from fear and guilt. Indeed it is probably the most difficult undertaking in life. Yet, the rewards are marvelous and wonderful.

I reassured him that if he was ready to accept this undertaking he would receive a tremendous gift, the gift of true joining – of being able to truly relate. Not only would he be able to relate better to White people, but to all people, particularly those that mattered to him. He could relate more intimately to his wife, his children, and to his God – for true joining helps us know that all things, people and events are related and connected at the deepest level.

V. Acceptance

Know That All Relationships Can Point To Oneness – Love

Harold continued to come to the sessions, sometimes filled with the excitement of a 3 year-old, but often showing signs of bewilderment and ambivalence, particularly about the new ideas we discussed. During one session, he told me he felt like he was taking two steps forward, three steps backwards, then sliding into a four-step routine. I didn't exactly follow his analogy, but I got the sense of what he was saying. I reassured him it was not unusual to have uncertain feelings. The critical judge in our heads was there to criticize and make sure we didn't feel like we were making progress. Our job is not to criticize the critic but simply let it do its job – criticize. Eventually, we will see it needs to criticize and accept it as just another companion with us on our personal journey. It has to come along for the ride with all the other mental companions.

"Yeah," said Harold, "but it seems as if the car is getting a little too crowded with all these extra riders."

I laughed and said, "The car is really a bus and there is room for all the complainers, the criticizers, the not willing one, the I am scared one, or the I don't think this is worth it one. They are welcome on the journey for they all want the same thing – to go home, like we do." Harold nodded his head, gave a brief smile and seemed reassured.

One day Harold came to a session in a huff. He slammed himself into his chair and before saying good morning uttered: "Women, they are so stupid! What do we need them for? They just create trouble and you can't tell them anything!"

"Well, good morning Harold and how are you and your wife doing?" I asked.

"Doc, don't you know about women? They are so fickle and they just don't think like a man."

As he made that statement, my mind immediately flashed to the scene in the movie, *My Fair Lady* when Rex Harrison sang: "Why Can't A Woman Be More Like A Man?" I quickly returned my attention to Harold and listened to him enumerate his wife's negative qualities and the difficulty that she was causing him. After several minutes of listening, I interrupted Harold with what seemed like a silly question.

"Harold, do you know that women are different from men?"

"Of course I know," he said. "What's your point? Are you talking about that *Men From Mars And Women From Venus* crap?"

"Yes and no. Beyond that which is obvious, it is clear that on earth, bodies are either male or female and the differences are not just differences – they appear to be opposite. Men and women appear to be opposite. In fact," I said, "the world is built on a principle of opposites and opposites appear to be separate. Up appears separate from down. Day is opposite of night. Front is different from back. Negative is indeed opposite of positive, and surely, good is separate and distinct from evil. That is the way of the world or so it seems."

"Yeah," agreed Harold, "that is just the way it is. Up is different from down and Lord knows women are different from men. That's good sometimes, but other times, it can drive you crazy."

"Yeah," I replied, "seems like different and opposite are the gasoline that runs this engine called life."

"Yes, so it seems, and is that also why we have all the trouble and misery?" asked Harold.

"Opposites ensure that there is separation and not only separation," I said, "but opposites often turn into something called opponents. Once an opponent is established, conflict, competition, and struggle must follow. For example, up does not struggle with down because up and down are content to be just that. Up is up. Down is down. No struggle. No conflict. No competition. However, once judgment is introduced into the picture, once we begin to think that one _is_ and _**should**_ be better than another, trouble enters.

Democrats are better than Republicans. Blacks are better than Whites. Men are stronger and better than women. Opposites are then no longer opposites. They become opponents and a hierarchy develops with all the ensuing struggles, be it struggle for power, position, pride or whatever. There is now a new component in the picture and that is one called "special". My side, position, or belief is better than yours and, therefore, I am not only different but also special.

The game has now really begun and becomes more complex and intriguing – for all types of scenarios and stories can evolve from this premise. And indeed it has," I said to Harold.

"So what," said Harold, "that's life. You accept it and deal with it. What's wrong with being special? What's wrong with wanting to be number one? I like to root for my favorite football team in the Super Bowl and I want them to win? So what's wrong with that?"

"Nothing," I said, "as long as you see it as that – just a game. Something that really has nothing to do with you as you really are. It is to enjoy, to have fun with but ultimately it is just a game. When we can see that life is just a game and that we are not defined by it, and that our true identity is not dependent upon whether anyone wins or loses, then we can know who we truly are and be free."

"Yeah," said Harold, "I can see that but that's hard."

"Of course it is," I said. "But that's hard because our mind must convince us that it is hard so it can maintain the misery and suffering in life. The three mental gods must make us think that there are opposites and they are not connected. The most basic way the mind accomplishes this is by making us believe in good and evil, thinking they are separate and not connected. The Truth is good cannot exist without evil for they are connected and one defines the other."

To illustrate this point, I asked Harold to give me an example of something that could be seen as good versus evil. He gave the example of Dr. King's victory over Bull Conner in Birmingham in the 1960's. "Clearly," he said, "Bull Connor was evil and if Dr. King had not won, neither you nor I could buy a hamburger at Woolworth."

"Of course that's correct, but Dr. King could not have 'won' if he did not have an opponent, Bull Connor. They were connected. They were joined in a series of actions. As opponents, they were not separate. We focus mostly on the differences between the two and not the collective actions that they were engaged in. Dr. King made Bull Connor and Bull Connor made Dr. King. The opponents were not just opponents. Their activities were complimentary. Evil is complimentary to good. They were opposite sides of the same coin. One could not exist without the other."

Harold seemed very reluctant to accept the point I was making. It was shaking the very foundation upon which he had built his life. In fact, he jumped out of his chair and exclaimed, "Man, you're crazy! You need to see a shrink! Not me."

I assured him that I was not his opponent and shared his sense of concern at the nature of my assertion. I told him that I was offering this to him not as unquestionable Truth, but simply as a consideration for him to ponder as we were delving into the nature and structure of the mind.

"Yeah, but this doesn't make any sense," he said. "God is good and Jesus was definitely good and the devil or Satan is evil and the two are not related. Anyway, what does this have to do with my feelings about my wife?"

"It has a lot to do with it," I said. "Your spouse is an opposite that can turn into your enemy if you are not careful. Your enemy or opponent or opposite has a tremendous gift for you, but you resist and fight them, which keeps you from experiencing the gift that they hold."

I reminded Harold that opposites only appear separate because the mind has a basic principle that everything in this world is separated. Separation is seen in everything, especially in relationships. One important way the mind sees others as separate is to see them as guilty.

"Your mind sees Bull Connor as your enemy and therefore guilty, Harold. Your mind sees your wife as your opposite and therefore guilty. Those that are not you and don't agree with you are seen as wrong and guilty. They become opponents that you need to be protected from and if the guilt is severe, the opponent becomes an enemy and can be attacked. You can attack Bull Connor even if it is only in your mind. Your wife can be attacked even if it is only in your mind. She is wrong and hence, she becomes your opponent – someone to resist – someone to fight against. Definitely not someone to join with."

"Projection," I continued, "appears to reinforce the belief that you are separate from another, for projection says, 'What I don't want, I place onto you.' If there is evil in me, I will not see it in myself; I will see it in you."

Harold quickly interrupted, "You mean like when Jesus said, 'Why see the mote in thy brother's eye and not the beam in thine own?'"

"Yes," I said, "Jesus was referring to projection. Projection also ensures that you and the other will always be connected. The other is carrying a part of you that you have not accepted because you have judged it bad, wrong and unwanted. Yet, you can't get rid of it by projecting. The guilt may appear to be in the other when actually it is in yourself. Attack is guilt projected outward. Projection does not rid you of guilt. It only appears to do so. The guilt still remains within you."

"Hold your horses, Doc," exclaimed Harold. "Are you saying Dr. King had evil in him like Bull Connor? Are you saying that I am just as guilty as my wife? If you are saying that, that's a big pill to swallow!"

"Of course it is," I said. "Maybe what I'm saying Harold, is there is a game going on called separation. Guilt is a big player in the game, and as long as we see anyone as guilty, it won't stop. Indeed, when we react to another and believe that he or she is wrong, we remain caught in a victim/victimizer game. We blame the other for our situation and feel as if they have done us wrong and are guilty.

In Truth, the other is simply showing us where our projected guilt is – the part of us we unconsciously did not want to identify with. Our judgments about them being wrong create the reactions that keep us stuck like a hamster running on a wheel. Maybe true forgiveness is not just saying to another that you forgive them. Maybe it is seeing that this is just a game of the universal mind with its three gods. Maybe it really has nothing to do with you – the True You.

Maybe that is what the Master Jesus knew when he cried: "Father forgive them for they know not what they do." He realized that the Pharisees, Pontius Pilate and others had projected their guilt onto him; a truly innocent one, and they did not know how their minds had tricked them. They were not aware of what was really going on. They were ignorant of the Truth and believed what the three little mental gods had told them.

They did not know the basic principle of projection, which is: one can only see in others what exists within oneself. The other is really just a mirror reflecting back to us what we have rejected within ourselves. If we can truly get this, and I mean truly, as in understand intellectually and at our core, then we will have taken a giant step toward releasing ourselves from the clutches of the three little mental gods.

"The gift," I said to Harold, "that is available to us if we see this mechanism is the ability to see all as good – a good that goes beyond the good that is opposed to evil. For we can then go beyond the world of opposites and see all as connected. Men and women are then truly joined and loved. Black and White can live out the vision that Dr. King spoke of in his *I Have a Dream* speech. That is the gift that others have for us. They hold what we have rejected. They hold what completes us. They hold what makes us All - that which makes us One.

Now, can there be a better gift? Our enemy is truly our lover. It is akin to the ancient teaching that says: if you can stare the devil in the face and see God, then your work on earth is finished. Once we see this Harold, the game is over, and we are one with The True One – The Infinite One. I, you and all others, and my Father are One."

VI. Acceptance

Be Willing To Question What You Think Is Real

Over the next few weeks, I begin to think more about my sessions with Harold. I realized, as his clinical psychologist, I was there to help him dive into the dynamics of his depression and anxiety. These conditions prompted him into therapy in the first place. I also realized that our sessions were going beyond the traditional psychotherapy sessions.

Although our sessions were psychotherapeutic, they delved into the nature of Harold's personal problems; they also seemed to have developed a life of their own. They were taking us into realms that many dared not go. Harold and I were asking some of the most basic questions about life, and I realized I was just as much a student in this learning process as he was.

As a member of the Georgia Psychology Licensing Board for twelve years, and as a past president of the Georgia Psychological Association, I was aware of professional boundaries and established psychological practices. I had no fear that these standards were being compromised. I knew as a practicing psychologist with more than twenty-five years experience that a therapeutic situation can sometimes go into unexpected areas. When that happens, unexpected events and results can occur.

I began to sense that not only was Harold on a spiritual journey, but I was on the journey with him, both as a guide, follower and companion. I became more reflective, and spent more time in quiet meditation. In fact, I began to reassess my personal, spiritual journey as a young Christian child growing up in Alabama.

Things were pretty clear and straight-forward for me at that time. The Bible was my guide and my authority. God was a masculine Power who resided in heaven, and heaven was some unknown place that clearly wasn't here on earth. When I became older, I wasn't as sure about the unquestioned authority of the Bible. Although I continued to read it, I had some reservations about the many different interpretations I heard from ministers about God and His expectations.

In particular, I wrestled with the concept of a God who forgave but nevertheless, believed in punishment. I began to seek other approaches to religion, and explored many non-traditional approaches to spirituality and God. From this, I surmised there were many untold paths leading to God, and we must find the path that brings us inner peace and love.

The primary belief I held onto during this process was "God is love." Although I wasn't sure exactly what that meant, I often translated it into a human relational context.

So, I thought if I treated my fellow man like I wanted to be treated, then I was approaching that which is of God.

I often said it was a pretty good way to think. It was nice and liberal and probably not offensive to anyone. It definitely was not offensive to God. After all, it seemed consistent with the two commandments that Jesus had spoken of when He said: "Love the lord thy God with all thine heart, soul, mind and strength, and love thy neighbor as thyself." Thus my primary principle stood on what seemed like pretty solid ground.

Yet, I kept hearing a nagging question inside my head. The question was so persistent that whenever I came to a conclusion about life or God or a spiritual teaching, I would hear, "Is this all there is?" This nagging question is what continued my inquiries. I knew that if Infinity existed, then whatever I concluded to be the final teaching wasn't.

Infinity has no boundaries, no limitations. Infinity does not have a limit. It cannot say this is all that you need to know, or this book or teaching is all there is. Quite to the contrary, Infinity does not know the word limit. No word or thought is Infinite, not even the word Infinity is Infinite. It is just a symbol of that which cannot be thought or grasped.

With this recognition, I knew that I not only must remain open-minded, but I also should be willing to question any thought, idea or concept, to determine if it was true, if it was real. Or, better yet, if it could point me in the direction of that which is real, true or Infinite.

With this understanding, I felt better able to engage in my discussions with Harold. Soon after I had this awareness, Harold called me and requested an emergency session. Normally, he would show up for his sessions on time, but never had he called me between sessions and requested to be seen as soon as possible. I agreed to see him, not quite knowing what to expect.

Harold told me he had been involved in an auto accident and needed to talk. I arranged my schedule to see him the next day, and he came to the session with a look of fear and bewilderment on his face.

He began the session by telling me that he was driving his car two days earlier. His wife was sitting in the front seat beside him when suddenly he looked toward his left side and saw a semi-tractor trailer truck advancing toward him at a high rate of speed. He tried to accelerate and swerve out of the truck driver's way, but was unsuccessful. The truck plowed into the back passenger's side of his car and demolished it. Harold and his wife survived the crash with only minor injuries.

He quickly added that it wasn't the crash that prompted him to request an emergency session. It was the way he experienced it that prompted him to call. He said when he saw the truck coming toward him everything around him began to slow down as if it was in slow motion. The truck, his car, his scream, his wife's movements, all seemed to be in slow motion. He said he actually saw it and experienced it. It was as if time and life had another dimension and what appeared to be a real situation didn't seem real.

I let him talk uninterrupted. He asked his wife if she had a similar experience, and her reply was "No." He then knew that it was his experience. He knew he could have been killed by the truck, and he was grateful that he wasn't, but he also knew something strange was going on that he didn't quite understand. As he talked about the experience, he became calmer and began to ask me some rather profound questions.

"Doc, how do we know what is real?" The accident made him question even the most basic elements we take for granted.

"Well, Doc, how **do** we know what is real? Do we believe what our eyes tell us, what our sense of touch or hearing tells us, or what others tell us? Is that it, Doc? Or, are we supposed to know through other ways?"

I asked Harold what he meant when he used the word "real." He wasn't sure, stating that he wasn't Plato or Einstein, but he assumed he meant that which is true or authentic.

"If that is the case," I replied, "then, maybe, we don't know what is real because Truth 'just is' and it may be beyond our grasp. Maybe what we think is Truth is simply our beliefs, which we are taught or we deduct from our senses. Either way, the bottom line is the Truth we think is real is actually only our thoughts, and our thoughts are products of our minds. In fact, they are just our minds."

Harold was somewhat bewildered by this response, but in his customary way he allowed me enough space to contribute to him. I explained that all the mind can do is think, and it thinks mainly from what it has been taught. In other words, the mind is always creating the past, although it seems to be the present. All thoughts are in the past. So, we never see anything as it really is. We see only the past and we judge what we think is before us from what we know of the past. The present never comes to us as the present.

"Wait one minute," said Harold, "I can't follow what you are saying. Are you saying I don't really know what I'm seeing right in front of my face?"

"Sorry to say, but yes. That is the case," I replied. "The mind sees something, and it has to identify it. To do so it refers back to files in its computer-like brain and labels what it sees before it. It then interprets the appearance. In other words, this chair that you are seeing before you can only be a chair to you because you have been taught that it is. You, therefore, identify it as a chair, believe it is a chair and everyone in this society would agree that it is a chair."

"But," I continued, "hypothetically, if someone from Mars saw this chair for the first time he would probably see it differently, because he has no computer file or conditioning in his mind to identity it as a chair. He has no concept of a chair. Who knows how he would see it, but he probably would not see it as you and I see it." Harold was quiet for a second or so, and I could see the wheels turning.

"I'm not sure that is true, but I'll go along with you Doc," Harold said. "If that is true, then that brings us back to my original question: how do we know what is real?"

"The best answer I can give you," I said, "is that we really don't know. The mind will quickly tell us what is real out of past conditioning, but we are just listening to a mind that only uses data from the past. It must show us a world built on limitation and separation that has a time/space dimension. For you, Harold, the car accident opened the possibility that reality is not necessarily time based. Even time itself is not what we think it is."

To explain further, I began to share with Harold a little of what I knew about quantum physics. Quantum physics raises the possibility that the physical universe is much more complex than we had originally thought. At the sub-atomic level, different laws of physics operate and create a reality that differs from what we are accustomed to.

Harold said he had also read a little about quantum physics and, like me, had avoided those hard classes in college. We laughed, but began to agree that there is a world and universe we don't fully understand, and we are lucky if we think we see only the tip of the iceberg called reality.

"Maybe," I said to Harold, "the two supposed realities of what we call the real world and what is often called the spiritual world aren't separate. Maybe it is only the mind, that mechanism that has to think and ensure that separate realities *appear* to exist, telling us what is real. If that is the case, we must question it. For how else would we know what is true, what is real, what is actual? The gift we can derive from this is a path toward Truth – a path that can lead to ultimate knowledge of what is really real. What else is there to do?"

Harold grew quiet and finally responded, "Nothing else, but I just don't understand all of this. It is so complex – so uncomfortable to consider."

"Yes," I said, "it is uncomfortable but maybe we have to keep in mind Jesus' statement, 'My Kingdom isn't of this world.' The Truth is found in His Kingdom, the real world is the Kingdom of God. Since we are open to the questioning process, maybe you and I can get closer to knowing what is real."

Again, Harold expressed some doubt and reservation, but finally said, "Let's go on Doc. I've come too far to turn around. So, what's next?"

VII. Acceptance

Stay In The Now

Harold came early for the next session, and I saw on his face all sorts of questions and concerns. In fact, the first statement he made as he entered my office was, "Doc, I just don't know. You left me hanging in our last session. At some level, I think you have something to say, but it is so confusing, so complex. You have to give me something more."

I knew what Harold was feeling, because I was feeling it myself. It is bewilderment and wonderment, coupled with fear and unwillingness to let go of what's familiar and comfortable for something that is unknown, mysterious, and even frightening. But, like Harold, I knew I could not stop, even if I wanted to. The journey was leading both of us to an unknown place, but we knew we had to go forward.

I was supposed to be Harold's guide, but at times I felt only one step ahead of him. Yet, I knew I had to trust a Guide that would get us to our destination, and I knew the path all too well. This Guide I knew was Infinite. Infinite and All love. All I had to do was be aware of my little three gods and ask the Invisible Guide to take charge.

Therefore, I responded to Harold's question with compassion. I let him know I realized he was uncomfortable, confused, and downright unsettled. I also realized he was a seeker of Truth. There was a part of Harold that he could not repress or deny. He said he always knew he would not be satisfied in life until he reached a place where he had no more questions. That place had to be a place of Truth. So, I asked Harold if he was ready to go to another level.

"Another level?" he responded. "What do you mean by that, Doc?"

I asked Harold if he was ready to challenge all his beliefs and psychological conditioning. I asked if he was willing to release them for other possibilities, for a world beyond the world he was accustomed to. He was ready and willing.

"I know you haven't forgotten the auto accident and your experience with time."

"Of course not," Harold replied. "It was as if time slowed down."

"The key words here Harold, are that it seemed as if time had slowed down. Your experience with time changed from what you are accustomed to. This experience, Harold, can give you the opportunity to see that all you believe is real is based on what you are accustomed to or conditioned to believe. All you know are your perceptions, and what you perceive is based on what you are accustomed to.

Perceptions, which include seeing, hearing, feeling, touching and smelling, are not accurate messengers of Truth. They only give messages that they have been trained to deliver. They are not accurate. We never see what is. We perceive what we have been taught. So, seeing is not believing. Believing is seeing. We see something, believe we know what it is based on our conditioning, and then we call it real. We never see it for what it is. We see it because we have been trained to see it as such. Remember the illustration of the chair in our last session?" I asked Harold.

"What does this have to do with time?" he asked.

"Plenty," I answered. "To know what is real, you must question the existence of time." Then I asked Harold to give me the time.

He looked at his watch and said, "10:15, Daylight Savings time in Atlanta, Georgia."

"How do you know this is true?" I challenged.

He looked at me and asked, "What's your point, Doc?"

"My point is that all time is made up. It is relative to where you are. If you are in another galaxy, time is not the same as being on earth in Atlanta, Georgia. Time, as Einstein said, is a relative concept, related to you and the place where you are. It is not absolute."

"So what?" Harold said. "I am not Einstein. I don't see what this has to do with my life."

I understood his position, but I explained if time is not absolute, then changing it is possible. Only Truth is absolute and unchanging. If time is not true, it can't be real. And if time is not real, and time is the way humans experience their world, then maybe this world isn't real!

"Now wait one minute," Harold said. "I'm willing to go out on the limb with you but now, you have jumped off into the Twilight Zone. Where is Rod Serling?"

I realized it was a huge leap, but when we seek Truth, we eventually must question what is real. We also must question the components we have been taught reality is structured on. We must determine if what we assume is real, is real. In particular, we must question such seemingly unquestionable concepts as time and space, because one defines the other.

"This is a lot to deal with, Doc. Are you saying that what I see, touch, taste, and so forth, is not real? Are you saying that, Doc?"

I remained silent for a few seconds and responded with a question. "What do you think is beyond time, beyond space, beyond perception? If Infinity exists, then there always must be something beyond what we know."

"Okay, Socrates," Harold joked. "I don't know. So, tell me."

"It is beyond thought," I maintained. "It is the unknowable, the unthinkable, the "just is". And if it just is, it is now. It knows no past or no future. It is. Now is beyond time, beyond space, beyond thought. Try to think of now. Can you do it?"

"No, I guess I can't," he replied.

"Now is eternal. It is Infinite. It is everywhere. Is there any place where it is not now? Is there more than one now?" I asked in a rhetorical manner. "Now just is, and it must be because it just is."

"Doc," Harold interrupted, "_**Now**_ just don't play word games with me, and that "now" I use is not just a pun. Seriously, you got to go slow with me. Are you saying that since we humans must think and act in time that we really are caught in a world that is not real? Again, I need to know."

I paused for a few seconds. "If now is all there is and now is beyond time, then what is really real? Maybe this that we think is real, is just a dream – just an illusion or just a trick of the mind. Maybe, it is just as a famous writer once said, 'a tale told by an idiot' and that idiot is the universal mind with its three little mental gods. And, the tale is always of separation.

The story has to have time and space in order to occur. It's the same old story – of one or a group feeling separate from their god and each other, always struggling but never really getting to that place of eternal peace. The human mind can't handle it. It is not in the cards. Eternal Peace can only be in the now. In essence time is like a movie scene where our minds are the projectors and the film is simply our life stories of separation, fear and guilt. The film is projected on the screen of time and space."

The room was silent for a few minutes until Harold broke in. "Well Doc, I guess you got something there, I think, but what does this have to do with me getting up on Monday morning and going to work, coming home to my wife, and arguing with her, and dealing with the White racists at work and in the world? Bottom line, Doc, what practical application does this have, or am I to sell my house, divorce my wife and move to a cave in Tibet? Come on, Doc, I got to earn a living. I got to function in this, what I think is the real world, even if it isn't real. What do I do?"

"Good questions," I said. "I guess it is similar to the statement Jesus left us with when he said 'we must be in the world but not of the world'."

"The best response I can give you Harold, at least for now, no pun intended, is also for you to realize that now is all we have and now is the only reality. Since it is the only reality, we really can't judge because all judgments are based on past teachings and conditionings. Therefore, we don't know who to judge or how to judge. No judgment makes sense, even what we call a fair judgment.

Judgments deny 'now' and hence, reality and therefore, perpetuate this tale of the idiot mind. But, since we seemingly are in the world, and I underscore the word seemingly, when we are faced with what we call reality, we should see it as a story. We should watch our minds make judgments and try to accept what appears to be happening with the knowledge that we will always interpret it to fit our story and rationale about life. Then we can allow ourselves to be more in the moment – in the now - and let that be an opportunity for the Invisible Source to show us what is really happening, what we are experiencing.

"This requires," I said to Harold, "us to be truly humble and allow ourselves to really not know what is real, what is true, and what is right. Out of this can come one of the greatest gifts imaginable, the gift of eternal peace and understanding. It is that peace that passes all understanding for it is beyond the knowing that the human mind can understand. It is the peace and understanding that comes forth when one is truly still. The mind, which believes it must think and move, becomes still and quiet, and we go to a place we know not of. When the mind is truly quiet, a "still small voice" can be heard. That voice can speak or impart the Truth and say, 'Be still and know that I (Now) am God.'"

Quietness took over the room and neither Harold nor I spoke for a few minutes. Finally, Harold broke the silence and said, "Tell me more, Doc. I got to know more about this unreal, real, or whatever you call it. I'll see you next session with more questions."

VIII. Acceptance

Know That The Invisible Is What Is Real

The more I reflected on my sessions with Harold, the more I realized all the training I received in graduate school, and my twenty-plus years of being a psychotherapist and college professor, could not have prepared me for the journey that Harold and I were traveling. All sorts of questions and self-doubts entered my mind. Was I going beyond the boundaries of traditional psychotherapy? The answer was obvious - of course I was.

I also realized that no profession could make progress if it isn't willing to push forward and go into uncharted territories. I felt a force within that was leading me on, assuring me that there was nothing to fear. Our goal was to find Truth that would not only set Harold free, but also me.

I found myself saying things to Harold that I couldn't explain. I didn't even know where the statements came from. All I knew was I had come too far to turn around. I had to trust this Invisible Guide that I believed was present in my sessions with Harold. This position is somewhat unusual for me. My academic training taught me to rely upon empirical evidence, or rational based theories - to know "that which is real". Even my religious background did not clearly define the role of an Invisible Guide, although it taught that there is another existence beyond that which we can see.

Yet, I felt uncomfortable in this new position of trusting an Invisible Guide, but I was focused on what I had to accomplish. Call it intuition; call it faith. Call it anything you want. It really doesn't matter what you or I call it. It just knows It is.

With this sense of assurance, I looked forward to my next session with Harold. When he entered the office, he again expressed confusion and reservation about our last discussion.

"Well Doc, you said a lot of heavy stuff in our last session, some of which I was able to follow and some of which left me with a big 'Duh' on my lips. You have to straighten this stuff out for me. In particular, you said last time that seeing is not believing, but believing is seeing. I don't know what you mean. Can you break it down to me in simple terms? I don't have a Ph.D., you know."

"That's fair," I said, "and I apologize to you if I got too far out on you. I'm trying to come to terms with some of this stuff myself. It is radical because ultimately we are asking if what we have known to be real, is real."

"Do we just throw away all that we think and have been taught?" asked Harold.

"Well, let's see," I said to Harold. "To fully understand what I'm saying, you have to accept as a premise that all we normally know are our thoughts. Our thoughts and feelings tell us what we think is real. Note I said, they tell us what we ***think*** is real, and we believe them.

Once we have this as a base Harold, we look out on the world and see a world that is consistent with our basic thoughts of life. That is why the grand dragon of the Klu Klux Klan can never see you for who you really are. He has thoughts about Black people that he thinks are true. He sees a Black person and then looks for evidence to prove that his thoughts and beliefs are true. He will look for ways to prove that you and I are inferior, and he will find them. This we called prejudice. However, the Truth is, we are all prejudiced. We all pre-judge people from our past conditioning. The K.K.K. is just an extreme example of what takes place with all of us."

"Now wait a minute, Doc", said Harold. "Are you calling me prejudiced? I marched with Dr. King during the civil rights era, and I am a religious man who loves everyone, almost everyone, at least. I try to treat all people fairly. Are you saying I, and even Dr. King, are prejudiced?"

"My point, Harold, is not to judge you or Dr. King, but to illustrate to you that the mind is like a computer. It makes us act according to the programs that are in our hard drives. We all are trained to judge, and we see a world consistent with our belief systems. We cannot be without our beliefs, because that is all the human mind is – beliefs. The mind's goal is to perpetuate its beliefs, especially cherished beliefs. The mind never stops judging on its own, Harold. For instance, you told me that at one time in your life you patronized nude nightclubs, right?"

"Well Doc", he replied somewhat embarrassed, "you see I was doing that for research purposes, you know?" He couldn't resist a hearty laugh.

"Regardless of what your motives were, and I really don't care what they were or what you did, my reason for bringing this up is to ask you if they had any fat or ugly women in these clubs? Did they?"

He seemed somewhat surprised at the bluntness of my question and responded with, "Well, don't you know, Doc? Are you a saint or don't you like to look at naked women?"

"Of course I do, Harold," I replied, "but my point is that someone, the manager or whomever, made a judgment to choose only what he considered attractive women. He knew that the men in the club would judge the women performing. These judgments would be related to the women's sexiness, their bodies or whatever. Your opinion and other men's opinions about the women actually prevented you from seeing them.

You just didn't see a woman named Carol; you saw a female body that you judged sexy. You were operating in your world that says, one is sexy or not, pretty or not. Yet, Harold, both you and I do it all the time. We don't see what's in front of us. We only see our judgments and our beliefs, and we think they are true."

Harold was in thought for a few minutes contemplating his new realizations and then stated, "Doc, if what you are saying about believing is seeing, then the extension of that is, we really never see what is real or true."

"Bingo", I exclaimed. "And it goes beyond that, Harold. Since we can't trust what we see to be real, and what we see is a result of what we think, then, maybe we don't really know anything that is real or true."

Harold's eyes widened. "Hold your horses there, Doc. You are laying a heavy one on me. You're really pulling the rug from under me, and everything I think and believe. That's huge. That's gigantic. That's Armageddon!"

At this point I wondered if I had gone too far, too fast with Harold. So, I chose not to respond immediately and went within for guidance from my Invisible Guide. A few seconds elapsed and I responded to Harold by saying, "I know this seems like a lot to swallow."

My desire was for him to at least consider the possibility that we really don't know what is going on in this world, or do we really know how to think, or what to conclude from what appears to be happening.

To illustrate my point, I told Harold that I wanted to share a personal story. "In the late 1970's I was brought to Morehouse College with the promise that I would eventually become chairman of the psychology department. I thought I had played the game correctly, but in two years I was fired due to a misunderstanding. At that time, not only did I feel hurt, I was angry and wanted to sue my alma mater for unjust treatment. To make matters worse, my wife was pregnant with our second child."

"Now pay attention Harold," I said. "I thought it was unfair, and my mind convinced me it was unfair. I was angry. No, I was mad with hatred. However, I made a decision at that time to enter private practice, because I did not want to work full-time for anyone again."

"Harold," I continued, "that was the best professional decision of my life. I am very happy being an independent practitioner. At the time, I didn't know what was best for me. I didn't have the big picture. I needed to be fired so I could get my freedom from being dependent. I had to leave Morehouse but didn't realize it at the time. I certainly didn't like the manner in which I was forced to leave, but the point is, I didn't know what was best at that time, and maybe I don't know what is best now."

"We just don't know what is best, what is right, what is true. We just have to let it be, and let life unfold as it must," I continued. "We just don't know – can you see my point, Harold?"

Harold again was very quiet and after a few seconds said, "Yes, I do see your point, Doc. I have a friend who had a similar experience and said the same thing. We just don't know."

"Acknowledgment of our ignorance can be so freeing," I said to Harold. "But we must be willing to go a step further. Are you willing to go with me, Harold?" I queried.

"Well, Doc, you haven't taken me to the nut house yet, although sometimes I wonder if you and I will have to run from the men in white coats, but who cares? Let's go!"

"Good and thank you for your trust and confidence," I replied. "The next question that arises is, if we can't trust our thoughts to tell us what is real, then is this that we call real, really real, or is it all a dream?"

"Now that's the sixty-four thousand dollar question, Doc," replied Harold. "Well, is this all a dream, Doc? If so, it seems more like a nightmare than a dream."

I smiled and asked him if he had ever had a really good dream? He thought about my question and stated that he had dreamed about his college sweetheart once. He was having sex with her and her old boyfriend caught them and started attacking him.

"That's good," I said.

"What do you mean, Doc, that's good? He was big, 240 pounds and 6 feet 4 inches tall. He was gonna tear me apart; thank God I woke up in time."

"That's good means that this dream is a perfect example to answer your question. In your dream, did you enjoy the sex with your girlfriend?"

He smiled broadly and asked if I had heard of his reputation while he was in college. I allowed him to brag for a while and then returned to my point.

"While you were making love in your dream, your body responded as if it was real. It had all the bodily reactions that you would normally have in lovemaking and your body didn't know whether it was a dream or not. In fact, the you in the dream didn't know it was a dream. It was only a dream, however, when you supposedly woke up and came to another level of consciousness, the level we call wakeful consciousness; the dimension we call real."

Harold quickly interrupted and said that this world is real because he can see it, touch it and think about it.

"Yeah, I know," I replied, "and therefore, that makes this real. But, weren't you also thinking you were doing this with your girlfriend in what you called dreaming? Did that not seem real to you? Didn't your thinking, seeing, and I know your touching feel real to you?" I smiled, as I questioned him.

Again, Harold was silent and I saw that he was really wrestling with these ideas. I left him with his thoughts, and finally he broke the silence by saying, "Doc, this isn't comfortable."

"I know, Truth will destroy human comfort. This **_world_** **_is not real_**. This visible, tangible world attempts to cover the real world, which is invisible. That which is real is invisible. Surely, you can admit, Harold, that there is tremendous power in the invisible. In this room there are radio waves, television waves and microwaves, which are not available to vision, to the human senses, and yet they appear to have power. We accept these forces that cannot be seen with the human eye as real. We therefore know and think that there is a reality that is invisible. We accept that as fact. But, if we say that God, Infinity is the only power, and God is spirit, then we must ask the question: is reality invisible?"

I knew what Harold was feeling. I knew the feeling when the rug is pulled fully from under your feet. It can be devastating. I told Harold that this was a very complex and unsettling place to be, at the very least, but I knew that he had to come to this place because he said he had to seek Truth, which can be quite upsetting.

"In fact," I said, "the more you enter the world of Spirit, the further you will remove yourself from the ways, means and thinking of what we call normal living."

A surprised look showed up on Harold's face, and he stated that he was concerned that he would be left with nothing, a scary place to be.

"No," I replied, " you can't be left with nothing if you are left with Truth because only Truth is true, and Truth is the only reality. The rest is just illusions. You will gain everything that is real if you stay open and humble. Knowing that only the Invisible is real will allow you greater freedom to operate in what is called the real world, the nine to five, go to work, earn a dollar, get in and out of relationships world.

This will give you the freedom to know that nothing in this world really matters, because nothing in this world has ultimate meaning or value since nothing here is true. Only God or Infinity is true. That is what I believe Jesus meant when he said, 'Seek ye first the Kingdom of God, and all will be added to you.' And, what is the Kingdom of God, Harold?"

"Right now Doc, I don't know anything. I guess it is safe to say the Kingdom of God is Spirit."

"Exactly," I exclaimed. "It is Spirit. It is Truth. It is Invisible. If you seek only that and realize that ultimately nothing here in this world matters, all that matters will be given to you. The gift, however, is not any material thing that may be or may not be added. This gift is: knowing your supply source. It is knowing that the Source of all supply is Invisible Spirit, an all loving Spirit. And, the true gift of knowing this, Harold, is indeed wisdom. It is a wisdom that all the great masters spoke of and anyone who seeks the Kingdom of the Invisible will receive this gift of true Wisdom."

In Harold's silence, I was beginning to see an emerging calmness and peace in his face that I had not seen before. After a few seconds, Harold replied, "Doc, I know deep in my heart that what you are saying is right and I want to get there. I just don't know if I can."

"Harold, we all can and will, because Omnipresence cannot be Omnipresence and leave you or anyone out. Think about that and we will pick up there in our next session. In fact, if it gets a little rough, you can always phone me."

He seemed more relaxed with my answer and said he really looked forward to our next session, and so did I.

IX. Acceptance

Be Willing To View Death Differently

Before my next session with Harold, I reflected over the many discussions we had and realized we had come a long way. We had dealt with some of the most important issues one could consider. I was particularly impressed with Harold's willingness to consider that everything he thought as real was, in fact, an illusion, a projection of his mind to keep the idea of separation alive for the three little mental gods. I knew this idea was one that most people considered foolish. Yet, Harold was willing to entertain the prospect that what most of us considered real was just an idea of the mind to perpetuate the insane notion that Infinity could have something separate and outside of Itself.

At some level, I believed Harold knew the insanity of the premise, but he, like most of us, felt there was overwhelming evidence that the world of the tangible seemed, felt and looked real. So therefore, it was real. To deny such, as he said, was insane. Yet, the contradiction persisted in his mind, and I imagined he had more questions for me.

However, Harold called before the next session to inform me that a distant cousin had died, and he was going to attend the funeral. When he returned, he naturally inquired about my thoughts on death. He asked if anyone close to me had died. I told him that my parents had been dead for several years.

"Doc," he asked. "Do you believe in life after death?"

"Life after death," I asked intuitively. "Let me ask you a question, Harold. What do you mean by death?"

A quizzical look appeared on his face, and in typical Harold fashion, he responded by asking, "Doc, have you been smoking those funny cigarettes or something? You know what I mean by death. You know, as in dying - no more oxygen, complete, finished, expired."

"If you mean the body, or form of an animal, dies, decomposes or changes form, then, yes, I believe in death. That is undeniable. But Harold, because a body dies does not mean that there is no more life."

"Now wait a minute," Harold said. "You have to give me more than this."

"Okay, I will. All things are born to live for an unspecified length of time. Then they die. That is what we believe. Let me ask another question, okay?"

"Well, I've come this far. So why not?" Harold answered.

"When and how will you know that you are dead?" I asked.

A few seconds passed and Harold responded, "I will know I am dead when I can see myself lying inside my coffin. But wait a minute; I see what you are saying. You're saying that if I can see myself lying in my coffin, then something must be existing inside me if I know that I am dead."

"Exactly," I responded. "That something, you can call awareness. That which is aware cannot die. You can call it soul or whatever, but it does not die. There must always be something that is aware, or who would know whether anything or anyone is alive or dead?"

"Okay, I see your point," Harold maintained. "I never understood this thing called soul, although they called me a soul man in my younger days. The ladies really said I had soul. They also said I knew how to touch their souls. Yea, I guess you could say I was really soulful, eh Doc?"

Naturally, Harold was smiling as he made these statements, and I let him relive his glory days for a brief while. Then I told him I agreed the word soul was used in many contexts and was often misunderstood.

"However," I continued, "what I really want you to see is that the mind must identify itself with a form. Every human being identifies with his or her body. It is our most basic point of identification. We know we have a birthday. We don't like to think about it, but we also know we have a death day. You think your body is you, and you think I am my body. In fact, if I were to ask you to identify yourself, you would probably go into your wallet, get your driver's license and show me a photo. You would say, 'This is me'."

Harold quickly interrupted, saying in his comical way, "And ain't I good looking?"

"Yeah," I said. "Save that for the ladies you want to impress. Yet, the key point in all of this, Harold, is the reason the mind makes you, me and almost all humans identify with our bodies as the basis of our identity is to ensure that its basic principle of the mind is established, not only established, but seen as unquestionably true."

"And what is that principle again?" asked Harold.

"That principle is separation. The mind must ensure that we all agree that the world is built around separation. The best way to do that is to convince us that we are separate bodies. I think I am Allen, a name given to a body born in 1945. You think you are Harold, born in the year of 1952. It seems unquestionably true and real."

"You see, Harold, the mind is very clever. The mind, which is the thought of separation from God or Love, had to make fear and guilt real, because Infinite Love or God is not fearful or guilty. The best way it could do this was to establish the belief that there is not only separation, but separate identities. These separate identities have form. The forms cannot last for eternity, because only Infinity or eternity is forever. These forms must decompose, must die. They will no longer exist.

"Once the mind does this, fear seems real. If you think you are this form or body, you will do almost anything to protect it from harm, death or non-existence. The body is seen as vulnerable, and as a result fear seems real."

"You mean like what Charles Darwin talked about in that survival instinct thing?"

"Yes, there is a fight for survival because there is a fear of not surviving. You are correct. So, it **seems** that the basic fear is fear of death."

"Wait a minute," said Harold, "What do you mean by seems? Is there a more basic fear than the fear of death?"

"Maybe, remember I said earlier that the mind must also have another basic emotion other than fear and that emotion is guilt."

"Boy, do I know about the guilt thing. My mama was good at using it. Even to this day, I can't do certain things because I hear her voice telling me that the devil is gonna get me because I did wrong."

"Yes," I said, "your mother was unknowingly acting according to the instructions of the universal mind and its three little gods making sure you could be controlled with guilt. Guilt is usually associated with something we as a body have done or not done. The mind will make a judgment and declare us guilty because of our actions or inactions.

This is especially easy for the mind to accomplish if the acts have anything to do with sex, because sex involves our bodies."

Harold nodded his head and said he knew exactly what I meant about the connection of guilt and sex.

"So," he said, "all of this identification with the body being us is to ensure that fear and guilt are real?"

"Yes and from this, we can have our life story. All of us, Harold, have a story of our life. It is a soap opera about our body interacting with other bodies around the issues of fear and guilt. That is the story of life, and it seems real because we think we are bodies. But, what if you were not your body? What would that be like and what would that mean?"

"Doc, the first thing I see is that I would not be a Black man or even a man. I wouldn't even be the son of my parents, a father to my children or a husband to my wife. I would not be any of those things. Everything that I am accustomed to defining as me would not be there. Then what would I be?"

There was quietness as I let him ponder the significance of this question.

"I give up, Doc," Harold finally replied. "Would I even exist?"

"Yes Harold, there would be existence, but not as you know yourself. You as Harold, the Black man who is a father, son, brother, and husband, would not be an authentic or real identity. The story of your life would disappear as a seeming reality. You would be able to see life differently because seeing yourself as a body would no longer be a reality."

"So are you saying, Doc," asked Harold, "that when I die, I won't see my mother or my grandmother in heaven, or God forbid, that no good boss of mine?"

"I'll let you figure that out yourself," I said. "But you must consider that if everything programmed in our minds is based on forms being separate from Infinity, then these are tough questions to answer. If the thought of separation is not real, then the world we see and believe in is not real, and it goes beyond that Harold."

"Oh no, do I have to dive for cover or are you going to hit me with a big bomb?" asked Harold.

"The biggest bomb," I replied. "If the thought of separation isn't real and the world we see is a trick of the mind to ensure separation, guilt and fear, then the personal identities called Allen or Harold also are not real!"

"Whoa!!" yelled Harold, "You've gone too far. I find it hard to accept that you or others aren't real. I will ponder that, but one thing I know is: I, Harold, am real. You better believe that or you're gonna have to take me to the funny farm."

I saw the distress in Harold's face. I clearly knew that he had been handed a lot. So, I was quiet for a while to let him relax.

Finally, he broke the silence and asked, "Doc, is this the last rug you will pull out from under me?"

"Yeah, at least for now," I answered with a smile.

I tried to be compassionate, as I knew this was a tremendous shock to anyone even if they trusted me. I knew he was having a tough time dealing with this discussion, but he persisted.

"Doc, I just don't know. These goes against everything I was taught and believe. Can you break it down to me slowly and gently?"

"Of course, Harold. Why do you think Jesus experienced conflict in the Garden of Gethsemane prior to his arrest?"

"Because Jesus knew he was going to suffer pain and die."

"You mean, he knew he was identified with his body and knew it could feel pain and then he would die?"

"Yes," said Harold.

"Doesn't it seem strange," I asked, "for a man to fear death or have conflicting feelings about death when he previously brought a friend of his, Lazarus, back from the dead? Don't you think he knew something about death that you and I do not know and would not react to death as you and I would?"

"Well, I guess that makes sense," said Harold.

"Perhaps," I said, "what was going on with Jesus was that he was not concerned about giving up his body and the pain associated with that. Perhaps, the struggle was giving up the mind, the belief that he was an identity with a form separate from God. Perhaps, his final surrender was to give up his identity to God with the realization that he and God were one and the same – a realization he had experienced previously but had not fully accepted.

Perhaps, he knew that his identity was not physical and definitely not mentally or psychologically based, but was spiritually based; an identity that has no limits, no bounds, no ends; one that knows no fear, no doubt, no guilt, no struggle, and has no need to fight for survival because it cannot die or know of death. Perhaps, Harold, this was his conflict and he fully resolved it, and knew that he could not be hurt because his Father or God could not be hurt. He knew that he was fully God or the Christ Identity."

A few minutes elapsed and he broke the silence and asked, "Doc, are you saying that even Jesus had self-doubt and fear?"

"No one can definitely say what was in the mind of Jesus. My mind is too puny and small to know or even to assume that I understand the mind of a Master such as Jesus. However, remember earlier, I said the mind has a greater fear than that of death."

"Yes, and what is that fear?" asked Harold.

"That fear," I continued, "is that we are all the same, hence not different, not separate, not individual personal identities with personal stories. That fear for us Harold is that we would no longer exist if we knew ourselves, because we would not be separate identities. We would not be Black, White, Jew, Gentile, Muslim, or even man and woman. We would be One and that One could not have any fear because it could not have any opposite or know of anything other than Itself. It could not know of differences. It would be All. It would be Love, a love that is all encompassing.

Harold, our greatest fear is that we are love and loved unconditionally, meaning no judgments, standards, expectations or differences. Separation would not be possible and the mind would not exist. We would be one. We would be love just because we exist. I am loved and love just because I am. Fear would no longer exist.

The gift that comes with this is truly a new birth, a birth into a realm that the mind knows nothing of. It is a birth into a realm that is all loving, without death. It is the gift of eternal life, a life that has no beginning or ending. It offers never-ending peace and rest. What could be grander than to know that all is well – to know of no conflict, war or struggle? What else would you want?"

"Nothing else, I guess," said Harold. "But boy is this a trip – one heck of a trip."

"Yes," I said, "but it is a trip toward discovering that which is eternal, that which is true, that which cannot end or begin because it is Infinite and eternal."

"Well," said Harold, "I guess I need a little rest. I've had enough to swallow for this session. I'll let this settle in and see you again next week."

As he was getting his coat, he asked in his amusing way, "Doc, do I go out the door or do I click my heels three times and just disappear into thin air?"

"Once you know who you really are and that you can't die, or even be born, then All is possible because All is real."

Harold smiled and left out the door.

X. Acceptance

Know That Your True Identity is Spirit

I sat down to reflect on my conversation with Harold. I knew that in this last session I had gone further out on the limb than I had ever gone before. I had taken him to a place where I believed Angels feared to tread. Harold and I had entered the place where reality was turned upside-down, inside out and stood on its head.

We had gotten down to the most basic premise of life. We concluded that the basic foundation of our existence, our bodies, were not real. Our beliefs led us to think we were something we were not. This confrontation would upset any normal thinking individual, and I was extremely grateful that Harold allowed me the space to introduce these ideas to him.

Yet, I knew this was a lot to handle, because it undermines the very foundation of what all believe. To confront someone with the possibility that the things they believed to be true actually were not true can be a mind-blowing experience. Not to mention that many individuals would not only feel threatened by such a confrontation, they naturally would resist it or even attack me for introducing such an idea to them.

I was concerned about Harold's reactions. I wasn't concerned as much about him being my client, as I was about the fact that he trusted me as a professional and as a spiritual companion and guide. My anxieties began to mount, and I retreated to my place of calm and peace.

I asked my Internal Guide, the High Self, for directions. As I was reflecting, I received a call from Harold's wife who said he was canceling our next appointment and would call me again to reschedule. Naturally, my initial reaction to this call was concern about our conversations and their effects on Harold. So again, I became quiet and listened for guidance from my Spiritual Source, my High Self. Peace eventually came over me, and I was released from anxiety.

A few days later, I received a call from Harold. He requested another appointment and indicated he had canceled the last appointment because he had to go out of town. He promised to give me the details in our next session. I hung up not quite knowing what to expect, but I was willing to remain in the mystery of life and let my Invisible Guide lead me.

When Harold came to the next session he walked into the room in an unusually slow and calm fashion. He remained silent when he took his seat, which was also unusual for him.

He finally broke his silence, apologized and said he was sorry for canceling the session, but felt an overwhelming need to get away and go to the ocean. He said water always calmed him, and his mind was in a state of turmoil after our last session.

Harold confessed that he didn't understand everything I said and finally, with exasperation he uttered, "Doc, it just didn't make sense at that time. I was scared to let go of all my cherished beliefs. I felt you had attacked all that I knew and held dear, and I wasn't going let you take that away."

I remained quiet and let him talk. He continued by saying, "I knew deep down that there was something to what you were saying. I just needed some space to sort it out."

"I understand," I responded.

"So Doc, I just went to watch the ocean, something I do occasionally to take my mind away. I was watching the waves come in and the thought hit me that the waves aren't really separate from the ocean. It is all ocean. The waves appear to have separate identities because the ocean is affected by the gravitational pull of the moon, or some scientific theory that explains why water in the ocean moves."

I encouraged Harold to continue.

"Anyway, Doc, I thought about what you said about life being a metaphor, and I began to see that the ocean could represent God. I realized we human beings are just waves on the ocean appearing to be separate from God and separate from each other, but the appearance is simply because there is motion in the ocean. Is that a rhyme? Am I a poet or what, Doc?"

A big smile spread across both our faces. I said with enthusiasm, "Yes, Harold, that is a good analogy. No wave can be separate from the ocean, as we cannot be separate from God."

"Yes," Harold interrupted. "I'm beginning to see and understand what you are saying. I, Harold, am not separate from God. I only think I am. It is my thinking that I am separate from Infinity, and identifying as this separate form that creates this identity and also this world for me."

As Harold continued to talk I could not help but think of the song from *My Fair Lady,* when Professor Higgins saw the break-through in his student and exclaimed, "I think she's got it!"

I let Harold continue recounting his discovery.

"The problem," Harold surmised, "is I am just identified wrongly. Not just me, but all of us. We think we are waves separate and apart from the source which is, in this case, the ocean. We even compare the size of the waves. I, as a wave, think I am bigger, better or smarter than other waves. In fact, my vanity and my arrogance become so real to me that I think I have power and energy that's separate from the ocean."

"In other words," Harold continued. "I think I, as a human, have power that's separate and apart from

Omnipotence. Boy, is that vanity? Is that insane? Are we all really this insane, Doc?"

Again I smiled at him and said, "Yes, it is insane to think that we would want to leave heaven and think we can have a power apart from the All Power Source. That, my dear brother, is the height and depth of insanity. Yet, that is what the human mind, with its three little gods, bases its version of reality on. In Truth, Harold, as you are so readily beginning to see, we have only one problem. And that problem is that we are misidentified. To use your analogy, our problem is that we identify as waves or individual human personalities, and not as the ocean or consciousness or Infinity."

"So what I see, Doc," Harold said, "is that as long as we think we have power separate and apart from God, we cannot go to heaven. Is that right, Doc?"

"Yes," Harold, I replied. "And the key word you said in this is 'thinking'. As long as we have a thought, which is a psychological activity, we cannot go to heaven because heaven is where God is and where God is there is no time or space. There is only here and now, and no human can think and be now. One can only be here and now. And now is beyond thought. Once thinking begins, we are in the past or the future, never now."

"As I see it," Harold said, "a wave can make a mistake. A wave can think it is separate from the ocean. It can identify itself as a form and think it is an individual wave, just as we humans identify with our bodies and think we are separate. But, I guess, it is like the question you brought up in the last session. What if we are not our bodies? What are we? What if a wave is not water in motion? Then what is it? Are we no-body? If so, then what are we?"

Harold was fired up. "Now here is the scary part, Doc. I really allowed myself to look into this."

A few seconds elapsed and I remained silent. "I guess we do have sacred cows, and this is one of our biggest," Harold surmised. "We dare not touch this one because it seems so real, so unquestionably real. Yet, I guess a wave that thinks it is separate, with separate force, is so unquestionably real, until it peters out and returns to the ocean like we all must do. So, much for the form of the wave, and, I guess, so much for the forms of humans."

"Very good," I replied. "The body not only keeps us believing in separation as it gives proof to the mind that we are separate, but it also carries out the mind's directive that we are special. My wave is better than yours, or your wave is bigger than mine. In fact, one or a group of waves may even assert that the ocean likes one wave or group of waves better than other. Some waves may want to struggle with other waves as they try to prove who is bigger or better. Does that sound familiar, Harold?"

"Sure Doc," he quickly replied. "All we have to do is pick up today's newspaper to see the battle of the waves. Stupid. Insane. I guess we are just stupid little humans wandering around lost, thinking we are some-bodies when actually we are no-bodies. And, the irony of it is, if we could see that we are no-bodies, we could be free. That is insane, isn't it, Doc!

"Yes," I said, "it is Harold, it is. "The universal mind with its three mental gods must make us believe that we are guilty and so, it tells us that we are incomplete, as in your analogy about the ocean. More accurately, we are incomplete without God. The universal mind tells us we have done wrong and are inadequate and guilty because we are seemingly separated from God. It tells us we disobeyed Him and will be punished by Him. Even though this is in our unconscious, it is always present and forms the basis for our every thought or action. As a result, we fear God and let our fear run our lives. It is the basis of all our soap operas, and yes Harold, you and I do have soap operas."

"Yeah, I know," said Harold. "I guess you could call mine 'As the Word Turns' in 'The Days of Our Lives' for 'The Middle Aged and the Restless'."

"That's cute," I replied. "You ever thought of being a comedian?"

A faint smile came across his face as he said, "Let's return to the scary stuff as I am really going to handle this deep, heavy stuff now."

"Good. You see, Harold, we are afraid of our unconscious because deep in our unconscious lies our greatest fear. Since fear only resides in our minds, essentially what we are afraid of is ourselves, our own minds. And, the paradox of this is that we cling to our minds. We believe our identity is our beliefs, our thoughts. So, we cling to these beliefs. Our fear is that we will lose ourselves if we give up them up. So we hold on and suffer with a few minutes of pleasure sprinkled here and there. We suffer simply because the mind tells us to or we will die."

"Now wait a minute," interrupted Harold. "I see what you are saying, but can't we be saved if we do good and follow religious teachings?"

"Who knows for sure," I replied. "But what happens, Harold, to the wave when it dies? Doesn't it return to the ocean? What happens to your identity each night, when you go into deep sleep? All we know is that the identity you think is so precious is apparently not there during deep sleep and maybe this is what happens in Reality."

Again a few seconds of silence passed, broken by a question from Harold. "So, Doc, what are we to do? Is there any hope?"

"Maybe," I said, "we are to reclaim our true identity and not continue to believe the false identity in our minds. The mind is the liar and it wants us to believe that we are incomplete, inadequate and have betrayed our Source. But remember, Harold, this is based on a thought accompanied by fear and guilt. Maybe what we must do is see these thoughts and emotions as tricks of the mind to keep us believing we are separate from God, Infinite love."

Harold interrupted and said, "You mean I can watch these thoughts and emotions like I watch the waves at the ocean."

"Exactly," I exclaimed. "Exactly! Once we do this, the thoughts will eventually die like the waves, and our true identity can emerge. We can be a quiet and still ocean of life. For our true nature is stillness, quietness. It is as the scriptures say, 'Be still and know that I am God."

"I got a better one," said Harold. "Wasn't it St. Paul who said, 'I live yet not I but it is the Christ that liveth within me.'"

"Excellent, Harold," I said. "It is the Christ, which is all love, and forgiveness; that you truly are. If you and I can know this, we will receive the greatest gift possible, for then, we will know who we truly are. We will have the knowledge of our true self – the true identity that is whole, complete and unlimited. This identity is all love. This, Harold, is what you are. It is what Jesus meant when he said, 'Be ye therefore perfect as your Father in Heaven is perfect.'"

"Yes," said Harold. "To know your true self is clearly the greatest gift that one can receive. And, I now see this is available to me. I agree that I am really the ocean and not the wave. I am greater than I ever thought I was. I am not personal. I am not physical. I am limitless. I am indivisible. I am invisible. I am Spirit. I am that and I am All. Thanks Doc."

"No," I said, "thank you. Well, I guess its best to say, thank God. Thank The 'I Am That I Am' – my real identity and in Truth, you will know that you are only thanking your Self."

"Yes", we agreed and smiled and Harold left smiling.

Epilogue

After Harold left our last session, I returned to my chair and began to reflect on our journey together. I recalled our early sessions when we talked about his depression and how it became apparent that he felt he was missing something in his life. Yet, he didn't know what he was missing.

He knew there was emptiness in his life that could not be filled with money, sex, drugs or booze. In exasperation, he finally asked a profound question: "Is this all there is?"

Little did I know this was the departure point for our journey, for that question opened the gate for us to leave the realm of traditional psychological discourse and enter the domain of spiritual seeking. I knew we could not leave the world of psychology altogether. Understanding the mind and the manner in which it tricks humans into accepting false beliefs and creating false gods is essential to any spiritual understanding.

Harold was a quick student in grasping the essential nature of the mind. Although he had been reared in a southern Black environment, and had accepted most of the values and teachings of his culture (the we-god), he was ready to learn more. Always in the back of his mind was that desire to find the answer to the big question: "Is this all there is?"

At some level, Harold knew there was more to learn, and it was this that released him from the attachments to his personal and cultural training, which up to now had held him in a stationary place. He saw that although these values were useful for their intended time and place, they had limited use and must be discarded once their usefulness ended.

I knew that accomplishing this task was no easy feat. There are so many pressures, both internally and externally, that pull us back to the familiar, to the known, to the comfortable. But Harold was able to face these pressures, both internally and externally, and proceed on his journey to Truth.

The journey, like most, wasn't always smooth. I introduced the "I Am" idea. Understanding "I Am" is absolutely necessary to come to Truth. Harold responded with wild astonishment and a great deal of confusion. He could not understand what I meant when I said that there was only one "I."

I took Harold back to Biblical scriptures and the encounter Moses had with God and the burning bush. God identified Himself as "I Am That I Am."

"Since God is "I" there cannot then be another. For God is Infinite, meaning all that there is, thereby leaving no room for another "I."

It is essential, therefore, to know that the only "I" is the "I Am That I Am." That is all.

Harold was able to see the logic in this, but his mind, like yours and mine, could not fully integrate this with the knowledge of his personal "i". That "i" is the root of all the problems that ever were, ever are and ever will be. The problem is believing there is a presence other than Omnipresence. There appears to be one big "I" that has all power, and six billion little "i's" that think they have some power. Utterly ridiculous, but this is man's way of thinking of his world. If man did not think, he would not have a problem. Man's only problem is that he identifies as a thinker.

It is psychology; it is the mind. It is the human thinking mechanism that must be investigated. It has to be exposed in its total nakedness for us to clearly know what is eternal, what is true. If it is not exposed, the mind will continue to try to distort Truth to fit the ideas of a personal "i" rather than allow that "I" that is "I Am" to be. The mind attempts to make up its own reality with perceptions, thoughts and emotions. Unless we understand these three psychological functions and the manner in which they attempt to distort Truth, we will never get to see what is real.

What really brought it home for Harold was returning to his religious roots and quoting Jesus who said, "My Kingdom isn't of this world." Harold knew this was true and he knew this meant another reality existed. This reality was not physical and not available to the senses. It was spiritually based. In other words, "My Kingdom" is invisible but yet, it is real. We have to go beyond the mind and its reliance upon perception to know the Kingdom of God. The mind cannot grasp this, but the mind, in its attempt to understand, takes what is the Kingdom of God and translates it into what it is familiar with.

For example, I recall asking Harold what he was taught about Heaven. He remembered his grandmother telling him it was a place with angels, who looked like humans with wings, and the streets were paved with gold. Again, it was the mind functioning to preserve its beliefs about reality, which was a violation of the First Commandment, "Thou shalt have no other gods before me." He was ***thinking*** he knew what was true. He was worshipping the false gods of the mind and not allowing the Kingdom of God, which is not knowable to the human mind. He was creating his own heaven or kingdom of God.

The concept that the "real" is not of this world was very difficult for Harold to accept. One day he asked, "If this world isn't the real world, then what is important here? Is there anything that is real, anything that is important?" I knew this was a very critical question. Since this world isn't real, nothing is important here. The only thing that is important is God or the "I that is I Am." Everything else is just stuff, just dream stuff, that the mind makes up to keep us busy in this world and distracted from God or the real world.

The Truth is only God, Truth, Love is important – nothing else. It is the mind's job with its three little gods to make us believe that something else is important. This mind if allowed will continue to control and dominate our lives, convincing us that life is built on differences and separation and All is not One but is composed of different forms.

Harold, like most, could not accept this initially, but I too had trouble with this concept. I remember a scripture that I learned as a child but did not fully understand then. The scripture was, "Pray without ceasing." As a child, I always thought praying meant asking God to do something for me. Although this form of prayer and other forms may be acceptable to some, I now know that if God is Infinite supply and all knowing, all that is His is ours. We have no need to ask. God being Omniscient – All Knowing - already knows.

All we need to do is have the conscious awareness of His presence. This means ignoring the clamoring of the mind with its three little mental gods and knowing that nothing here is important. Only the Kingdom of God is important. That is my only function and thus, the only important thing in life. That is praying without ceasing.

You may ask the obvious question, "What of my job, my family, my church – aren't they important?" Only because you say they are. But, be cautious. I am not saying you shouldn't do those day-to-day activities. Do whatever you need to do to function in this so-called real world. Do what comes next but meanwhile, pray without ceasing knowing that only "My Kingdom" is real.

By this time, Harold was accustomed to my rather shocking pronouncements and did not reel in horror. Yet, he was not fully comfortable. He had to get to the point where he knew what he was reacting to was the personal "i", which was supported by the we-god and the creator-god – all idols within his mind. He had to know he would always react to his mind and his emotions, which act to prove this world is real. The two emotions that are the most powerful in doing this are guilt and fear.

Every human feels guilt. The belief in sin or guilt is essential to the functioning of the "i" that thinks it is human. The key is understanding the mind cannot tolerate too much guilt, so it always looks for others to project it on. Others are to blame, particularly those the mind judges to be our enemies. Our enemy is really just a repository for our unconsciously projected guilt. Our enemy carries what we do not want to claim or identify with. He is an opposite who has turned into an opponent and threatens our safety and security.

The Truth is, we are so psychologically connected to our enemies that we dare not even look at them unashamedly or without guilt, for fear we will discover that our enemy and we are one and the same. Harold thought white racists were his enemies, but they were simply people he projected his guilt onto. They kept his attention focused outward rather than within. Jesus asked the question, "Why do you see the beam in your brother's eye but not the mote in your own?"

If the Israeli's could see the Palestinians are not their enemies or vice versa, then they could see that they are truly one. Jesus teaches us we should love our enemies and do good to those that despise and abuse us. As long as we think we have an enemy or opponent, we will see ourselves as humans and not know that our true identity is spiritual – the "I that I am." "I Am" is not Christian, Jew, Moslem, Buddhist, Black, White, male or female. "I Am" is All, beyond any form or concept or belief. That is why loving your enemy is actually loving yourself. In Truth there is no other. There is only One.

This, of course, is too threatening to our personal identity, so we live in a world where we have opponents and enemies. We even have a god who has an opponent – the devil. If our god can have an opponent to defeat then we, as humans, can be justified in attacking and trying to defeat our opponents. Why do you think competitive sports are so popular all over the world? Someone must win, which means, someone must lose. A victory must be proclaimed. It is just another way our minds keep us in the world of drama and stories. And, it is a story with very predictable results.

Harold could not accept these ideas initially. Yet he persisted. He kept asking questions. In one session he asked about guilt and fear in a rather defiant way.

"Well, Doc, if there were no guilt what would people be afraid of? Wouldn't they just go out and rape, rob, steal, and kill without the fear of God? They could just do what they wanted to do without fear of consequences. Don't we have to have laws with consequences?"

I remember feeling somewhat boxed in by these questions because they seemed so reasonable. The answer has to have two levels, as there appears to be two separate levels of existence. At the level of the human mind, the six billion personal "i's", there is a need to have laws, rules and consequences. People have to be held accountable for their actions. If they break the rules, they must pay a price. They made an error, but they are not sinful. They are not guilty.

At the level of spirit, none of it is real. Remember what Jesus said to the woman who was caught in adultery. He knew she had broken a law and told her not to do it anymore. But he also said, "Neither I condemn nor persecute you." He saw error, but he knew judgment and condemnation keep us caught in the mind without love. Love accepts without any standards. It is unconditional like the Father's love for his son in the story Jesus told of the prodigal son. The father was not concerned with the acts of his son. He just wanted him to return home and was joyous when he did. And this is the case for you and me.

When we return home to the Father; when we realize who we truly are; when we know we are spirit and not psycho-biologically based entities, then we can return home and enjoy the feast that is awaiting us. We must let go of our fear and guilt, which keep us in the pig-pen like the prodigal son.

This was a breakthrough for Harold. I could see his face beam and he said, "Yeah, I really want to go home to my Father's house."

Actually, we have never left. It is like Dorothy in *The Wizard of Oz.* This is just a dream. And, all we have to do is awaken from it.

"But, how do we do that? Do we click our heels three times, like Dorothy. What do we do?" asked Harold.

That is the question of the ages. To awaken from the dream you must know that there is only one and that One is I – the "I that I Am." That is All. Sounds simple but it is not so easy.

Everyday you must see others as not guilty. They may make mistakes as you and I do, but they are not guilty. We all have difficulty and problems but we are not sinful. We have simply erred – made a mistake. This is a step toward forgiveness.

Another step towards true forgiveness is appreciation of everything in our life. Our minds tell us some things are good and some are bad, but in The Kingdom of God, all is good. There is no bad. Appreciation pulls the rug out from under the mind's need to judge because judging has to have right and wrong. Without judging, the mind begins to deflate and become impotent. The final thing we can do is to know only God is Truth. Only God is real. I don't mean the concept of God we have been taught.

We must become open to all that is unknown to us. We must know that we do not know what is really true. In other words, we must be willing to know that we are totally ignorant or unaware of all that is so. Our minds will attempt to tell us we are wrong but we must be committed to be open to all that is Infinite, Love or God.

Clean out your mind. Go inside and see the workings of the three little false mental gods. Know they have no power

except what we give them. Then stop, listen, be still, hear the voice of quietness and know that "I Am That I Am." I am All. I am Love. I am You, because there is no other. There is no you. Ultimately, we will see there is no we, because "you" is just a concept of the mind. To make a world outside of us seem real, which makes the idea of separation seem real. The idea of "you" is the most insane idea that the mind conceived. Omnipresent is incapable of having anything or anyone outside of It. It is All Presence. All Knowing. That is the I that is I. I Am is **not** personal nor is it physical. I Am Invisible. I Am Spirit.

At this point, Harold and I knew the journey was over. It was a journey without distance because it was a journey to our True Selves. It was the Alpha and Omega. It had no beginning or ending.

I smiled, sank back into my chair and thanked God for sending me Harold and realized that I can only thank me or "I Am" for in Truth there is no Harold. There is only the I Am. I realized I was at peace, at one with All – not I, Allen, but I, The Christ, who is One with the Father, the only I there is.

About the Author

Allen Carter received his B.A. from Morehouse College and his Ph.D. in Clinical Psychology from Columbia University in New York. He completed an internship in Clinical Psychology at the University of California Medical School in San Francisco, California.

Dr. Carter has held terms as past presidents of the Georgia Psychological Association, the Georgia State Examiner of Psychologists (Licensing Board) and the Atlanta Chapter the Association of Black Psychologist. He has also held several Board and Committee positions in the American Psychological Association. Currently, he is in private practice in Atlanta, Georgia and serves as Director of Clinical Services for the Morehouse College Counseling Center and is an adjunct professor in the Psychology Department.